Life's Biggest Questions

Life's Biggest Questions

Mark Vincent

The Christadelphian
(on behalf of the Christadelphian Auxiliary Lecturing Society)
404 Shaftmoor Lane, Hall Green, Birmingham B28 8SZ, UK

2017

First published 2016
Reprinted 2017

© 2017 Christadelphian Auxiliary Lecturing Society

ISBN 978 0 85189 363 1 (print edition)
ISBN 978 0 85189 364 8 (electronic edition)

Printed and bound in the UK by
Short Run Press Limited

Contents

1. Too much information 1

2. What's your point? 4

3. The longing 8

4. I think, therefore He is 11

5. Grand designs 15

6. God or chance 18

7. The artist 23

8. Something to say 27

9. The prime directive 31

10. A two-fold duty 34

11. Something's not right 38

12. Under construction 41

13. The human conundrum 45

14. The 'S' word 49

15. A brief history of sin 53

16. Eureka! 59

17. The 'Good News' headlines 62

18. The golden thread 65

19. New leader 68

20. No ordinary man 70

21. Ministry and message 73

22. The crucifixion 76

23. The greatest gift 80

24. Resurrection...84

25. Kingdom come 89

26. On earth as it is in heaven 92

27. The return of the king 95

28. The to-do list 99

29. Belief.. 103

30. Saying sorry 107

31. Brand new start... 110

32. Passport to the future...113

33. New family 116

34. Time to get ready 121

35. Next steps...125

Appendices

  1. The authority – the remarkable credentials of the Bible 130

  2. Further information...137

Chapter 1

Too much information

THROUGH a strand of fibre-optic cable no thicker than a human hair you can pump data at the mind-boggling rate of 90,000 telephone directories per second. That's a crazy amount of information – each one of those directories might contain 700 or more pages and 400 lines of data per page, and imagine a room stacked with 90,000 of them! It's an almost incomprehensible amount of information, and all of it potentially coming down that hair-strand fibre pipe every second.

It's a powerful metaphor for the way in which we're swamped by data in today's society. We're practically drowning in it – to the point that it sometimes feels overwhelming just trying to keep up. The average daily newspaper today contains more information than a person in the seventeenth century would come across in their whole lifetime. Doesn't it sometimes feel that it's just too much? There are too many irrelevant facts, too many opinions, too many 'experts' – in short, too much data, not enough wisdom.

What do you want to know today?

When you think about all the information we have access to today a question presents itself: how much of this information is actually *useful*? – the kind of thing that you would really want or need, as opposed to mere noise? Let's try a simple exercise for a moment. If you type 'How many bones in the human body?' into your phone the answer is spat out in milliseconds. (It's 206 – interesting, but unless you're a doctor, does it really matter?) 'What's the largest organ in the human body?' (It's the skin, followed by the liver.) It seems like you can know anything you want to know – the only limit is your imagination and the extent of your questioning.

Or is it? While the internet is great for trivia (and for much more besides, of course) there are some questions it's not so good at. Suppose you now type 'Why am I here?' or 'How should I bring up my children?' or 'What's going to happen to me when I die?' None of these are trivial or unimportant questions, but suddenly the information age doesn't seem quite so effective. Of course there will be lots of material online about each of these topics – sites galore, in fact. But which will you trust and how credible will the answers really be? Frustrated, one might well go back to using the internet for more mundane data gathering, booking some tickets, perhaps, or finding some juicy celebrity gossip.

But let's not leave those big questions to one side too hastily. What we've got here is a real and serious problem. Isn't it true that it's those big questions of life, the 'whys' and the 'hows', which are the really important questions that we *ought* to know about? These, surely, are the questions which truly matter and which we *should* be able to answer, yet we rarely get time to even think about them because there's too much to do and there's so much other trivial information getting in the way. We may even have given up on such questions as being too hard or too controversial (the sort of questions that students might debate at three o'clock in the morning when those of us with jobs or families have gone to bed). Yet it is these questions which address the very essence of who we are as human beings and what we are meant to be here for. It would be ironic, wouldn't it, to know precisely how many bones there are in one's body or the nature of the proteins in the brain – or to devour every fact about a favourite football club or preferred TV star – but not to know if there is any meaning, point or purpose to one's life?

Three questions

Perhaps at the end of the day there are three really big questions. These questions relate to past, present and future, those three slices of time through which we see the world. We can make them personal to ourselves as individuals like this:

- Where did I come from? (my origins, my past)
- Why am I here? (my present purpose)
- Where am I headed? (my future)

Or we can think of them with respect to human beings as a whole like this:

- Where did the world come from? Is it a random accident or a purposeful outcome?
- What are human beings for? What is their point and their place in the world? Is our story part of a larger story or just a random accident?
- What future is there for society to look forward to? Where is the world going?

These are the questions we will be discussing and hoping to answer during the course of this book. They are not theoretical questions, because each of them has really practical outcomes which can positively affect – even drastically improve – the way we live life each day. These are the really big and truly fascinating questions of life, questions which, if we can only answer them satisfactorily, have the power to transform a human life and fill it with meaning and purpose.

Chapter 2

What's your point?

AT some time or other *everyone* wonders about it. Even rock groups write about it, for all their fame and fortune. Here's Queen, for instance, writing not long before Freddie Mercury's death back in the early 1990s in their song, 'The Show Must Go On':

"Empty spaces – **what are we living for**?

Abandoned places – I guess we know the score ...

On and on! **Does anybody know what we are looking for**?

Another hero – another mindless crime.

Behind the curtain, **in the pantomime**.

Hold the line! Does anybody want to take it anymore?

The show must go on!"

There can be a huge emptiness in life, when we take the time to stop to think about it, driven by the fact that many people are confused about what life is *for*. Is it just a huge play, a farce, a pantomime with no lasting significance? And if it is, *whose* show is it and before whom are we performing? Is it right that there really is no meaning to any of it, so that the best thing one can hope for is chance?

"Whatever happens, I'll leave it all to chance.

Another heartache – another failed romance.

On and on ... **Does anybody know what we are living for**?

I guess I'm learning

I must be warmer now ...

I'll soon be turning, round the corner now.

Outside the dawn is breaking,

But inside in the dark I'm aching to be free!"

Those last lines capture this longing for something more, for freedom from the shackles of the inevitable 'show' that must be lived yet cannot be fathomed.

But is life really so absurd? Can we not do any better than this?

Is 'stuff' enough?

One common approach is simply to dismiss these questions as being either too difficult or possibly even unanswerable. Instead we might busy ourselves with activities of one sort or another in an attempt to ignore the emptiness and the lingering questions of our existence we might otherwise feel. We might well seek to fill our lives with as many enjoyable activities as possible while the going is good, making hay while the sun shines by indulging ourselves as much as we can.

This may seem all very well for a while, particularly when times are good, but unfortunately those times don't always last. Besides, merely having more things and enjoying more experiences is increasingly proving to be a bankrupt exercise. It seems that we're built with this insatiable appetite for something more, but when we try to make that 'something' material possessions ('stuff') – or if we make it the pursuit of pleasure or self-indulgence – we only find ourselves empty again, with the ultimate fulfilment that we crave still beyond our grasp. There's an old saying that there are two disappointments in life: one is not getting what you want, and the other is getting it. It is a bizarre paradox that if we are lucky enough to get just what we want we can find that it does not give quite as much pleasure as we had thought it would – or at the very least, that our old problems have not gone away. The pursuit of self as the goal of life does not really work in producing any lasting kind of satisfaction.

We sometimes tell ourselves (and advertising is *always* telling us) that if only we have this thing or that – this car, that handbag, this spa treatment, that lifestyle – then we would be *truly* happy. But while we may indeed enjoy the experience and be happy for a short time, the promise never really brings the fulfilment it seemed to offer. At the end of the day the materialism that so much of Western culture is built upon fails to pay up on its promise; we never end up looking or feeling as good as the person on the advertisement, and if by some miracle we do, we'll soon take it for granted and end up feeling as though something is missing once again. There's a reason why psychologists have begun to talk about what they call 'post-purchase depression' (PPD for short) – that feeling of emptiness when we've bought something and the novelty starts to wear off so that pretty soon we have to look for something else to bring satisfaction. The amassing of more 'stuff' around us won't fill the sense of emptiness and the need for purpose that can exist in the human heart.

And, if we think about it, neither can many other activities. No matter how much we enjoy golf, we will never be able to play enough rounds to fill a human heart. No matter how much we throw ourselves into our work or whatever hobbies we pursue we will find that ultimately they are not sufficient in themselves to make us truly happy. If we pursue hedonism, living as if the more beer or shots we drink, sex we have or parties we go to the happier we will be, we shall still find ourselves unfulfilled. As one writer once put it, the quest for a 'higher high' will either end in failure or kill us.

Stuff versus relationships

It's clear, then, that stuff (whether physical objects or activities and experiences) is not enough. In fact merely the title of a best-selling book makes the point effectively: the book was called 'Stuffocation'. The very things that we think will liberate us can end up taking us prisoner and causing us to suffocate.

Perhaps the answer is that true happiness and purpose are to be found in *relationships* rather than possessions and experiences. We are getting much warmer now in our quest, but we are still not quite there. Even human relationships are only *part* of the answer because even they can never completely fill our hearts. Why is that? Because wonderful though they are, they too bring disappointments and have all kinds of shortcomings. Even if we make what seems the more noble choice of making some other person or relationship our 'centre' or purpose – our children, say, or our partner – we can end up being cheated or disappointed, or we can lose them. What will our purpose be then? Even the most wonderful human relationships have their limits in terms of how much another person can truly understand us; there is a sense in which ultimately we are alone. Forging good relationships and bringing joy and kindness to others is certainly a central *part* of our purpose, but as we shall see in the next chapter, there is another aspect of relationships which must accompany it.

In short, there must be more to it than the merely here and now. People seem to have within themselves a spiritual longing and a longing for eternity which craves to be met but which is too often ignored. World history is littered with people who have sought to find happiness and fulfilment by having *more* – more power, more culture, more status, more land, more wives, more children, more friends, more possessions, more fun. Some of these people have been able to call on massive resources in order to pursue their goals. But they have never really found the satisfaction they sought – it *always* eludes. Every day millions more are engaged in the same experiment – 'if only I have *more* of whatever-it-is then everything will be all right'. But the fulfilment they crave is always around the corner. As a religion (for that is what it has become), materialism and the pursuit of happiness centred in oneself has failed.

Chapter 3

The longing

AT the heart of human beings there seems to exist a longing, an emptiness, an unmet desire, a sense that 'there must be more to life than this'. What is this longing and why do we have it?

C. S. Lewis, the author of *The Lion the Witch and the Wardrobe* and the other Narnia adventures, thought this question was terribly important. He wrote about a 'God-shaped hole' in the hearts of men and women. The reason why we experience this emptiness, he argued, is because there is *meant* to be a place in our hearts for God, and if we try to replace that space or fill it with something else, the emptiness will always remain. So yes, relationships are crucially important, but not just relationships with other human beings; we were also made for a relationship with God and not purely for ourselves. We were simply built that way, designed for Him. When we ignore Him, there will always be this sense of something missing. As human beings we have a spiritual capacity – the need for a spiritual relationship with God – just as we have the need for emotional relationships with other human beings. If we don't address that spiritual potential, if we don't find a way of meeting that inbuilt need, then our lives will always be something less than they have the potential to be.

Living towards God

There seems to be a higher purpose, then, to human life. We are meant to live *towards God*, and when instead we live only towards or for ourselves, it's small wonder we are frustrated or left feeling a little bit empty. The Bible says that we are made 'in God's image'. This means that we are meant to reflect Him and are meant to engage with

Him. It's our destiny and if we don't take it up we fall short of what we have the potential to be – fully actualised human beings in His image.

Imagine you have a tool designed for one thing, perhaps a spade meant for digging – but instead of using it for the purpose for which it was designed you insist on using it for something else, perhaps as a cricket bat or as a broom to sweep the yard. There's no wonder you would end up frustrated and perhaps disillusioned if you tried to use a spade for those purposes, wondering why it doesn't work so well. It *sort of* works (one can just about imagine hitting a ball with a spade, or using it to scrape together a pile of leaves) but it's clearly not what the spade was designed for. Now if you put it to work digging the garden instead you would suddenly find it a much more acceptable piece of equipment – you would have found its purpose. Just as the spade is designed for its purpose so we were designed for ours: to live in relation to God as well as in relation to other human beings. When we insist on applying ourselves purely for our own ends or otherwise attempt to remove Him from the picture, things simply aren't going to work properly in the long run.

There is thus a 'why' and a 'for whom' to our existence, a point and a purpose behind it all. When we don't live in tune with this purpose, that's when problems start. The emptiness is felt because we were designed for something more than the here and now; when we ignore that destiny it's not surprising that there is the sense of something missing, something out there which we can never quite reach.

The leap of faith

This all sounds very fine, you may be thinking, but we have just made an awfully large assumption here – that there even *is* a God in the first place. We may be able to see that there is something missing – this emptiness and this endless quest for something more or something *other* – and it may be a wonderful or comforting *notion* that we might have a higher purpose, a God to whom we belong. But is it *true*?

And how would we possibly know? Is the notion of the existence and presence of God just a feeling that some people have, whereas others don't? Is there any rational basis for believing in God, or is it the case that science has long ago made Him redundant? The longing for God and the search for a higher purpose seems to fit very well with what we know of human longing and experience and answers a great need that humans seem to have felt throughout their various civilisations over millennia, but is it just a projection of our wishes rather than reality? Is belief in God still credible today?

This brings us to a question which is absolutely fundamental and which we must pause to consider in the next few chapters. If we can answer it successfully – that is, if there is a God – then this will lead logically and naturally to some very powerful answers to those big questions of life with which we began.

Chapter 4

I think, therefore He is

AND so to the biggest question of all: is there a God? Believing in chairs is easy – we can see them and touch them and so we 'know' they are there. But believing in God is not like this because we don't see Him – we only see the indicators of His presence. But what are these indications, how can we spot them, and just how compelling are they?

A glass and a universe

One line of evidence is to think about the universe and where it might have come from. [1] For many centuries and even millennia it was common to believe that the universe was eternal and so did not have an origin to be explained. With new discoveries – many within the last hundred years – scientists now almost universally recognise that the universe had a beginning (it is quite interesting in this light that the Bible's very first phrase in Hebrew is 'in the beginning'). When we think about this beginning it's not just a question of where the 'stuff' came from – the matter and the energy out of which the universe is made; it is also about the 'why?' of it – why should there be anything *at all* (rather than nothing). There might also be a 'who?' question – is there an *agent* or force behind the universe which is required to bring it into being?

---

1 Another approach would be to consider whether there is evidence for God's activity in human history. Believers point to examples like the evidence for the resurrection of Jesus, or the fulfilment of very specific Bible prophecies in subsequent history as making a compelling case here. Indeed there is a lot of evidence supporting the Bible's claim to be a supernatural book, which of course implies the existence of some kind of superior power or God (see Appendix 1 – page 130).

These questions are entirely legitimate and correspond exactly to the sort of questions we ask about much simpler objects we come across in every day life. A glass of water on the table beside us, for example, can be explained not only in terms of its atomic composition but also in terms of who made it, why they should have done so, and why someone would have put it beside us. What no one would accept (I think) is that the glass of water 'just happened', 'came out of nowhere' or is simply there 'for no reason'; there is almost certainly a very good reason for it, in terms of the *where from*, the *who*, and the *why*.

Now if all this makes sense in terms of the glass of water, what would happen if we applied the same questions to the universe? We could ask where it came from, and we could ask both in terms of the stuff that makes it up (where did the matter and energy that it contains come from?), and in terms of the *agency* behind it (*who* or *what* caused it to come into being). We could also ask about the *reason* behind its existence, the 'that for the sake of which' it is here.

If we would not accept that the glass of water 'just happened', 'came out of nowhere' or is simply there 'for no reason' why would we accept this about the universe which is so completely full of things that have causes and reasons of just this type?

Cause and effect

The very discipline of science proceeds on the basis that we can work backwards from effects to causes, that we can ask about the stuff of which we, our planet, or even the universe is made and that we can then work back through time to earlier states which explain the present one. But no matter how far we go back along those lines we won't really have got anywhere with the much bigger question of how and why there is *anything at all*. Where did matter, energy, space and even time itself come from? For that we need to go *beyond* matter and *beyond* nature (to something *super*-natural, in other words, which starts to sound like God). At some point we need something outside matter to explain matter because matter can't cause itself. [2] Indeed, the universe itself had a beginning. This means that the universe itself seems to need a cause *outside of itself* to bring it into being because it cannot cause itself.

Julie Andrews summed this up rather well in *The Sound of Music*: "Nothing comes from nothing, nothing ever could." It really is as simple and as logical as that. We can't explain matter *by* matter or nature *by* nature, space *by* space or time *by* time; what we need to cause the universe is a *super*natural cause – something acting outside nature, beyond space and time and thus able to bring about the conditions for it to form.

Some propose that this cause might be just an impersonal force rather than a personal God, but we have absolutely no indication as to what that force might be, why it should exist and why it should have acted. [3] Sometimes it is thought that the laws of nature themselves require the universe to come about – that the universe is an inevitable consequence of their existence. But this only pushes the question one step further back: where would those laws have come from, if indeed they had such power? Laws do not invent themselves; you need a lawmaker (a rational intelligence) to explain the existence of these laws since they are rational rather than random or chaotic. The laws of nature cannot sufficiently explain the existence of nature in just the same way that the laws of chess don't explain the existence of chess – you need a person and the concept of *mind* if you want to explain chess, and it would seem to be the same for the universe. We need something outside the system, and most likely something beyond an impersonal force, to cause and explain the beginning of our incredible universe. We need something on the order of a supernatural mind.

---

2   Otherwise we end up in an infinite regress. It's also worth noting that what does not exist has no power to bring anything else into being.

3   A more technical argument is that an impersonal force would have acted infinitely long ago and by the process of entropy we would correspondingly all have disappeared infinitely long ago as the sun burned itself out.

The choice

Think of it like this. Essentially we have a choice. One option is that we have a world – in all its incredible expanse, intricacy, beauty and complexity – which came about by an incredibly unlikely chance: for no apparent reason, by no cause, by no one and for no one. Under this scheme the only explanations we have access to are *material* explanations (explanations grounded in matter), and *natural* causes; there is nothing immaterial, nothing outside nature to which we have recourse which can explain how the world would have come about. If that is the case then all the world's order, beauty and apparent design mean nothing; the universe is but a random fluctuation in infinity, as are all our lives – there is no cause, no meaning, and no purpose. It is all chance, and it is all meaningless. That is one option.

The alternative view is that there is something outside nature – something *supernatural* which has caused nature and even time and space itself to come into being. Fascinatingly, the God we meet in the Bible is exactly the sort of uncaused cause, the necessary Mind beyond the material, the unmoved mover beyond time and space, which we need to account for the 'problem' of the universe.

Chapter 5

Grand designs

O VER the last couple of decades TV programmes about house design and renovation have become massively popular. One of the aspects of human nature they pick up on is that we all have some sense of style and design, although quite clearly some more so than others! If we scale this up from individual homes to a larger level, we instinctively know the difference between good design and bad design or chaos – the difference between the Taj Mahal and a rubbish dump, the paintings of a master and the scribblings of a child – and we know that good design requires a designer.

Principles of good design

Whether we think at the level of the universe with its myriad galaxies and stars, at the level of our planet with its incredible landscapes and diversity of life, or whether we go to the microscopic, atomic or sub-atomic level – at each of these we see the most amazing 'effect' that we could possibly imagine. What could possibly have caused such an effect? What kind of designer could have designed on this scale and at all these levels? This would not seem to be the effect of an impersonal force or of an accident of infinitesimally small probability. This is the effect of a master planner, a designer, a being attuned to beauty, intricacy, laws and morality. While forces and tools are used to build buildings, great buildings require great architects and designers – beings with personhood, mind, aesthetics and values who plan and scheme and have a sense of the magnificent. The universe is the most amazing building ever built and the evidence is mounting to an extraordinary degree that it was made 'just so'.

Scientists – in particular physicists and cosmologists – sometimes speak of the 'anthropic principle' when discussing the uniqueness of the universe. There are a number of scientific constants (we can think of them like control dials which seem to define and constrain our world) and which, if just one of their values were changed by an extremely small amount, like one part in a million or even one part in a million million, would render the formation and existence of the universe and life completely impossible. The question is, why is it that these 'dials' have been set at these highly specific values to enable the stable existence of the universe and to enable life? It is as if something or someone *wanted* there to be a universe containing intelligent life and set the dials accordingly. It's only in the last fifty years that scientists have come to appreciate just how extraordinarily unlikely it is that this would have come about by chance. Indeed, they sometimes speak about this phenomenon as the 'Goldilocks principle' – just as Goldilocks' porridge was neither too hot nor too cold but just right, so it is with the universe – but *why?* The concept of a designer who 'pre-tuned' these conditions and set the dials seems highly plausible.

Here are two illuminating quotes from Stephen Hawking on all this:

"The odds against a universe like ours emerging out of something like the Big Bang are enormous. I think there are clearly religious implications."

"It would be very difficult to explain why the universe would have begun in just this way except as an act of a God who intended to create beings like us." [1]

Hawking himself apparently does not believe in God, but it seems he can see the logic of faith from his scientific research if these comments are anything to go by.

---

1   Stephen Hawking, quoted in Francis Collins, *The Language of God: A Scientist Presents Evidence for Belief* (Free Press, 2006), page 75. Both are cited in Tim Keller, *The Evidence for God* (Dutton, 2008), page 130.

Probabilities

Of course it *might* all be a coincidence – this could be a possible explanation. But it would seem to be an extraordinarily unlikely one. We are not just dealing with the improbability of *one* extremely unlikely thing happening by chance, we are dealing with the cumulative improbability of *all* the individual steps happening by chance including the production of matter, the formation of galaxies and planets, the precise conditions on our planet that seemingly uniquely enable it to sustain life. Then on top of this the processes of chemical and biological evolution would need to happen for us to get here by accident.

We are dealing with the colossal improbability – if not impossibility – of *all* these things, each element of which is massively improbable. But we don't need just one of them to happen, we need *all* of them and each at exactly the right time and in exactly the right way. If there is a world where blind chance is all that operates, would one really expect this kind of predictable, intelligible world in which we live? Can one look at the world and really say that it has come about because of a massive chain of lucky accidents?

Chapter 6

God or chance

WHAT type of cause would you need to cause a universe? First, the cause would have to be external, most probably a supernatural one as we've seen – something outside nature which can bring the whole thing about. If we are in a universe which operates according to laws and logic, a universe which is predictable rather than chaotic, then this suggests something about the type of cause that would have brought it into being and points us in the direction of intelligence rather than purely an impersonal force. We would need a rule-maker with intelligence to explain the origin of that rationality.

Believers are sometimes criticised as being believers in a 'God of the gaps' – gullible people who allow science to explain as much as possible, and then call God in when they get stuck. But this criticism is all wrong. It is the very fact that we *can* understand so much – the rationality and logic of the universe – which requires an explanation! If the world is all blind chance, why should it have so much order and meaning rather than tending to chaos? It is the very intelligibility of the world which speaks of a supreme Intelligence standing behind it. Why? Because things which are intelligible are the product of intelligence. A thousand monkeys sitting at typewriters randomly hitting the keys do not produce the Complete Works of Shakespeare no matter if you give them all eternity to do so. Intelligibility in the universe (the fact that we can in a measure understand it) arises because there is intelligence behind it. If there were no God then in the extremely unlikely event that there were anything at all we would be scarcely able to comprehend it in the beautiful way in which we can.

Signs of mind

There are other pieces of evidence which suggest a supernatural intelligence or mind behind the universe. We could think, for instance, about the data in our DNA, the data which specifies other creatures and the parameters of nature. If I have a USB stick or a hard drive with data on it, the data got there because I (or someone) put it there; it didn't spontaneously generate itself. Why, then, should we accept this for the data of DNA? This data is non-random (the test scientists have set as a criteria for potentially identifying extra-terrestrial intelligence), so it is unlikely to have spontaneously generated itself out of nothing. Instead it bears all the hallmarks of intelligence. Where did this data come from? Don't we need an Intelligence to explain it?

When we think about human beings it becomes even more apparent that their cause must be more than an impersonal force and must instead bear the attributes of mind and personhood. We are naturally impressed by the size of the universe, by the number of stars and such like – but the bigger miracle may lie within us. A human brain has more connections between its neurons than there are stars in the galaxy. We have a whole set of capabilities (aesthetic, emotional, psychological, spiritual, intellectual and relational) which completely distinguish us from other forms of life. Why should this be? Is it really just an accident or could it be that we have these capabilities because we reflect our Maker? The best explanation of mind and personhood (surely the most interesting thing *within* the universe) is that there is a greater Mind and Person whom they reflect.

This would also explain why people look for (and often find) a sense of purpose, meaning and morality in the world. They look for these and in some measure find them because they correspond to a real need that we have as human beings, a need which can find its resolution in the One who made us. It would explain why we have an aesthetic sense and relational and spiritual qualities which transcend the merely material. This is why music makes us dance or why art achieves the emotional or aesthetic impact it is designed to provoke.

We do not need these things for survival; we need them because we were intended to aspire to be like our Maker.

Expectations

In concluding these chapters about God's existence it is an interesting exercise to turn the whole question on its head. What we've done up to now is to start with our world and think about the possibilities of where it might have come from, arguing that the existence of God is the most likely explanation. Another approach is to start with the God described in the Bible – the supernatural mind of which we've been speaking: just yet merciful, creative and artistic, moral and righteous, all-powerful and wise yet supremely loving. A God who longs for obedience and worship yet gives free-will because He does not want forced worship. A God who seeks harmony and reconciliation in the world, and longs to be in a deep and fulfilling relationship with it. We can then ask, if such a God were to exist, what kind of world we would expect to see. We can think about this in the form of a checklist:

We would expect to find:

a world of order and consistency, with set laws and patterns	✓
a world of astonishing beauty, vastness and complexity	✓
fine-tuning suiting the world for life	✓
an attractive, well-equipped place or home where creatures could exist	✓
a world containing free agents (humans) with tremendous capacities (intellectual, creative, relational, spiritual)	✓

a sense of morality and responsibility amongst those humans	✓
human-derived problems (particularly when God is rejected) and the sense that we should do better	✓
humans with a massive conundrum at their core (they are uniquely like God yet they share the fate of lesser animals)	✓
human ability to overcome their animal instincts to make decisions according to a higher purpose	✓
an inability of humans to find ultimate satisfaction with the material	✓
the possibility of deeply fulfilling relationships with others and God	✓
a sense that there must be a plan, a future, a purpose, a meaning	✓

There is a remarkable correspondence between the world we would expect to find under the Bible's assumptions and the world we actually do find. Simply put, it fits.

By contrast, if we start with the assumption that nature is all there is, that mutation and natural selection is the 'whole show' and that our existence is, as C. S. Lewis once put it, but "a senseless contortion upon the face of idiotic matter", then we should expect to find none of these things: no order, no beauty, no scale, no purpose, no morality, no music, no art, no religion, no society, no humans, no creatures, no life, no planets, no universe. Nothing. It is possible that the astonishing 'something' of which we are a part is really a nothing (that it has no meaning and it is not going anywhere other than a sticky end when the sun burns out). It is possible to believe that this great 'nothing-masquerading-as-something' came from nothing. But it seems hard to imagine a less convincing explanation.

Far better to conclude, as most people in the world in fact do, that there is indeed a God, a higher intelligence and guiding, creative mind who is responsible for us all and in whom we have our origin and highest goal, our beginning and our destination. This, then, would be our solution to the 'Where do I come from?' question – I come from Him and I am here for whatever purpose He made me for. Let's go ahead, therefore, and find out just what that purpose is.

Chapter 7

The artist

WHY do artists draw or paint? Why do musicians play or composers compose? For anyone with a strong artistic drive these are not even questions – the answer is so obvious: creative people simply *have* to do it because it's part of who they are. It is an irresistible impulse which cannot be denied and requires no reason; it is what artistry and creativity demand. It is the outward expression of who an artist is.

The greatest Artist

If we can relate to this artistic drive (even if we don't necessarily have it ourselves) then we can perhaps start to grasp something of God's reasons for creating the world and the scale of His artistry. For a being *so* creative, how could He not create?! It's an interesting fact that in the Hebrew Bible (the Old Testament) the verb 'create' is used many times, but only ever with God as its subject. It is as if creativity defines who He is. By contrast, as creative as human beings undoubtedly are, their efforts at creativity are more akin to the rearranging of pre-made objects in comparison to the true creativity of God. The whole world – from the vastness of the galaxies to the wonders of each and every human brain – is but an expression of who He is.

The book of Psalms – a collection of 150 poems and songs to be found roughly in the middle of the Old Testament – expands on this point:

"The heavens declare the glory of God,
    and the sky above proclaims his handiwork.
Day to day pours out speech,
    and night to night reveals knowledge ...

> Their voice goes out through all the earth,
>   and their words to the end of the world." (Psalm 19:1,2,4)

God's creative work is described as an act of communication from Him – a message of self-expression which tells of who He is. The creation is like a book whose message from God we can 'read' no matter what language we happen to speak. There are times when, as creatures, we just need to 'get out there' into the incredible world that He has made and feel the awe and the wonder of it as a way of bringing ourselves closer to Him and listening to what He has to say.

Character and relationships

There are also some other helpful ways of trying to understand God's purpose in creation. One is to think about God's character or personality. There is a fascinating Bible passage in which God describes what sort of a God He is. It begins like this:

> "The Lord, the Lord, a God merciful and gracious, slow to anger, and abounding in steadfast love and faithfulness, keeping steadfast love for thousands, forgiving iniquity and transgression and sin ..." (Exodus 34:6,7)

The passage goes on to talk about other aspects of God's character such as His standards and His judgement which are equally important, but for now let's just stick with what we have so far. If this proposition is true – that God really is a God of mercy and lovingkindness – then this has some tremendous implications. Every one of these qualities are attributes which are *relational* – that is to say, they involve other people and they necessitate relationships. You cannot love or be merciful by locking yourself in a room and hiding away; you cannot show forgiveness or lovingkindness in a vacuum – you need other people in order to show all of these qualities; you need relationships. Only then can each of these wonderful attributes come to life.

This means that God was compelled – if we dare use that term in speaking of Him – to create the world (and in particular to create human beings) in order to give full expression to who He truly is.

A world which seems perfectly appropriate for human beings with emotional, spiritual, aesthetic and relational qualities so that they can interact with Him is exactly the sort of world we would expect if God is the God the Bible says He is. The whole creation, and especially our particular part in it as human beings, is the natural expression of God's character and perhaps the only way He can be who He truly is.

A bigger message

We would expect that a God like this would not content Himself merely with creating the world but also that He would care about it and interact with it. It would be completely untrue to His character to put the universe in motion like some giant wind-up toy and then simply watch and wait as its future unfolded. The picture the Bible presents is of a God who is intimately involved with the world – involved, even, in the affairs of human history and in drawing them to a great conclusion.

Nor is God finished with communicating with us just by virtue of the physical world He has created. There would be no point in creating human beings who in some measure reflect Him only to leave them to fend for themselves with no input from Him – not if the whole point of creating them in the first place was to enable such relationships! We would expect Him to interact and we would expect Him to communicate.

It goes without saying that human beings have an almost insatiable desire to communicate amongst themselves. When our regular tools of communication such as eyes and ears are damaged in some way (whether through accident or injury) we go to incredible lengths to find workarounds so that we can still communicate. Communication seems to be fundamental to who we are – we simply *have* to do it; it's part of what makes us human.

What though of God? Our reflections on Him so far have already brought to light His genius of creativity and His artistic expressiveness. We've seen Him as the great source, the mind our minds so imperfectly reflect. If we are indeed made in His image as seems to be the case and if communication and relationships are so intrinsic to who we are, wouldn't it make sense that these capacities reflect His own?

Indeed they do. The very sort of God that we require to explain the universe is precisely the sort of God who would have something to say to us and who would want to engage. It's only logical that such a God would have spoken. But where can we find out more about all this? If it makes sense for God to engage with His creation, how can we find out more about those engagements and what His ultimate plan really is? That is where the wonderful story of the Bible comes in.

Chapter 8

Something to say

B Y His very nature God is expressive and communicative. He has spoken, not just in a general way through the world He has made, but also in a much more content-rich way. He has told us who He is, what He is like, what His plans are and how they involve us. He has told us about ourselves – where we came from, what we are doing here and what we can hope for for the future. And He has done so in the Bible.

The one and only

The Bible is a book which is absolutely unique among the literature of the world; there is quite simply no other book like it. It is one of only a handful of books in history which have claimed to be the word of God, but it stands far apart from all of them because of its track record and unique characteristics. More than eight hundred times the Bible informs its readers that it is recording the very words of God Himself, not only educating us but also explaining to us God's actions through history and His amazing plans for the future. It has remarkable credentials to back up these claims such as a whole set of specific and detailed predictions of events made many years before but which have subsequently come to pass. These prophecies which detail some of God's interactions in human history are on a whole different level in terms of their specificity and predictive power when compared to other purported 'prophecies' such as the vague writings of Nostradamus, for example. A flavour of some of these unique credentials of the Bible (including a few more details on Bible prophecy) is given in Appendix 1 (page 130).

The good news that arises out of this is that we now have an authority to which to turn. God has not left us in the dark on these big questions of life; we do not need to speculate, nor to resign ourselves in defeatist fashion to the possibility that we can never know. Nor to accept the trite but obvious untruth that all truth is relative – that there are 'many truths' or 'many paths to the same end' (how can this be so when those paths are clearly mutually contradictory?).[1] By contrast, God has spoken clearly and powerfully, just as we might have expected Him to – and He has done so in the pages of the Bible. This doesn't mean that there is no disagreement about what the Bible says; clearly it needs to be interpreted. But to anyone who reads the Bible with an open-mind, free of prejudice and preconception, a surprisingly clear and liberating message emerges.

The trouble with experts

Without this we really would be all at sea because we would be forced to listen to fallible human 'experts'. Even for relatively mundane questions like daily health and diet there are so many different and often contradictory voices that we end up bewildered and confused. One study tells us red wine is good for us, and the next month another study comes along that says it isn't. How can we really know for sure?

---

1   The claim that truth is relative – that there is your truth and my truth but they are merely different roads to the same place – sounds like a very attractive idea. Under such a scheme there is room for everyone and we can each have our own opinion while retaining a warm fuzzy feeling that, while we may be on slightly different roads to one another, they all ultimately lead to the same happy destination. But when you really think about it, this makes no sense. All of the major belief systems of the world (including atheism) make truth claims, and these claims must be either true or false – there is simply no two ways about it. For instance, either the world and all we experience within it is the result of blind, pitiless chance or it is not. This is not something which can both be true and not true. Either it is possible for us to be reincarnated when we die or it is not; this belief is either a truth or a lie – it cannot be both. Either Jesus Christ is saviour of the world or his claims are those of an impostor – and so we could go on. These are all truth claims and none of them can be simultaneously true and not true. If we are to be intellectually honest there is no option but to examine the evidence and make a choice.

We might turn to science, especially given its excellent track record at understanding how the world works, fighting disease, sending people into space and so on. But it is not the domain of science to tell us how to live, nor to teach us about God (even though there are many scientists who believe in Him and find their research supportive of their belief). Science may tell us many things about *how* or *when* the world came about; it may offer remarkable insights about our surroundings and how things work. But it doesn't begin to tell us *why* there is a world, and what it is *for*. It doesn't tell us anything about *how* we should live and *why*. That's simply not its remit.

Politicians are not going to help us with our big questions either, and what of experts such as sociologists, psychologists, philosophers or religious leaders? While they may certainly have some fascinating things to say it turns out in the end that they can only offer so much. Sometimes their answers are uninspiring or unsatisfying, but an even bigger problem is that their answers are simply contradictory – how can we know who to believe? Faced with this dilemma what are we meant to do – simply pick the answer we like best or the one that sounds right to us? The very idea makes a mockery of there being any real answers or absolute truth. Furthermore, our trust has been breached too many times by those who make claims but whose personal lives have contradicted their message. We have seen too much hypocrisy from politicians, religious leaders and 'experts' of one sort or another making it hard to trust any other human being on these questions.

In contrast to all of these alternatives, the ability to go to the Source of everything – the God of heaven Himself through the pages of His word the Bible – is a tremendous and reassuring opportunity. No human being, no matter how well-educated, sophisticated or cultured, has the right to say authoritatively what the world is all about, when even the most well-informed person is fallible and can only know a tiny fraction of what there is to know. As knowledge of all kinds continues to grow explosively there are more and more specialists in esoteric areas, but it becomes harder and harder to bring it all together and see the big picture. Who is really qualified to talk about the reason for *everything*? Surely only the One who brought it all into being in the first place.

Releasing the mask

We began an earlier chapter by quoting a Queen song. Here's another which draws together some of the things we've been discussing and raises a further question:

"If there's a God or any kind of justice under the sky
If there's a point, if there's a reason to live or die
If there's an answer to the questions we feel bound to ask
Show yourself – destroy our fears – release your mask."

God has told us that there *is* a reason; there *is* a point. But we won't find it by navel-gazing, by listening to politicians, psychologists, scientists, or other 'experts'.

There is an answer to the questions we feel bound to ask. Though it might be difficult to hear Him in the midst of all our noise and that deluge of information we thought about in chapter one, the fact is that God is not silent, and He isn't wearing a mask. He has the answer, and He has told us what it is. So now let's take a closer look at just what God has to say with His unique message recorded in the Bible as our guide.

Chapter 9

The prime directive

A S the world's best-selling book of all time, the Bible opens in grand style with the following announcement about God:

"In the beginning, God created the heavens and the earth."

(Genesis 1:1)

So in the beginning (whenever and whatever that was), there is God. The Bible is about God. The world is about God. The world is about God because He made it and it is a reflection of Him, an expression of His abilities and power as God. Its purpose is whatever purpose He has with it, because He is in charge.

God first

This is critically important – it's important for understanding the Bible's world view, and it's important for understanding our own role as human beings within that world. We are created by Him and are subject to Him. The world is not about you or me first and foremost – it is about *Him*.

Yet within that scheme of God creating a world which reflects and manifests His character and personality, human beings have a significant role. With our unique and superior abilities, human beings have been given a key leadership responsibility in the animal kingdom. They are to be stewards or managers, so to speak, acting on God's behalf in the world He has created. This is their job, and it is described like this to Adam and Eve as God addresses the angels at creation:

"Then God said, 'Let us make man in our image, after our likeness. And let them have dominion over the fish of the sea and over the birds of the heavens and over the livestock and over all

the earth and over every creeping thing that creeps on the earth.'
... And God said to [Adam and Eve], 'Be fruitful and multiply and fill
the earth and subdue it, and have dominion over the fish of the sea
and over the birds of the heavens and over every living thing that
moves on the earth.'"   (Genesis 1:26,28)

Two essential points are made in those words. The first is that
human beings are in God's image and so share a relational affinity
with Him, a potential to be in some way as He is. The second, stated
twice and at some length, is that God is delegating the day to day
management and responsibility for the earth to men and women. This
is quite an honour when you think about it. Any sense we might have
that humans have got to the top of the supposed evolutionary tree
because of their own ingenuity or good fortune is transformed into
the idea that we have been put in a position of enormous privilege by
God, a privilege which brings with it enormous responsibility.

Unfortunately mankind as a whole hasn't done a very good job
at this management role. Given the environmental issues facing the
planet and the uneven distribution of resources within it (to mention
just two examples), we can conclude that man's story has to some
extent been one of mismanagement rather than good stewardship.
That, though, is a story for chapter 11 and beyond.

The grand plan

Whatever the mistakes human beings have made, this doesn't mean
God has given up on His plan or the original directive that He gave.
He still wants a world which reflects His character, expresses who
He is, and gives honour to Him. He still wants human beings to play
a significant part in bringing about that future world. It is put in the
form of a mission statement in one of the early Bible books. It sets out
God's ambition for His world:

"But as truly as I live, all the earth shall be filled with the glory
of the Lord."   (Numbers 14:21, KJV)

So that's it: the great secret of everything – God's 'mission statement' with the earth, the 'why' of it all. In the corporate world companies have increasingly recognised that they must have a purpose, a vision or mission. But the significance of these mission statements pale in comparison with the mission statement of God's purpose just quoted – the great reason for everything. It's so important, in fact, that we should quote it again:

> "But as truly as I live, all the earth shall be filled with the glory of the Lord." (Numbers 14:21, KJV)

Just as an artist might take a canvas and seek to paint the most exquisite picture he or she is capable of, or a composer might set out to create a great symphony, so God is engaged in creating a world which is full of His glory and splendour, a world which speaks of His infinite creativity and wonderful character – a world which reflects, manifests and communicates His glory and His nature as God.

Now this mission-statement or promise on God's part is no haphazard or random thought. It has *always* been God's purpose, and on another two occasions in the Bible God sets out exactly the same agenda:

> "... For the earth shall be full of the knowledge of the LORD as the waters cover the sea." (Isaiah 11:9)

And again,

> "For the earth will be filled with the knowledge of the glory of the LORD as the waters cover the sea." (Habakkuk 2:14)

This is about as succinct an expression of God's over-arching purpose as there could be. It is the prime directive: God plans to fill the earth with His glory. It is an entirely good thing, not because God is egotistical but because His glory is amazing and He wants to share it. He wants to share Himself with the world He has made and be present within it. The world is to be an expression of His glory.

Chapter 10

A two-fold duty

IF God's plan is to fill the world with His glory and our role within it is to be good stewards of what He has made (so that this glory can be revealed), then we are already some considerable way towards understanding our own purpose (or 'why') as human beings. But is there more that could be said? It's time to think a bit more about the purpose of life from a human perspective – what would God's 'user's guide' to being a human being have to say? Is there more we can understand about our responsibilities so that we can come to live more in tune with our creative purpose?

God and neighbour

Why don't we look at how Jesus himself summarised the primary duty and calling of human beings? In one of his most famous teachings he summed up both what God wants from human beings and what a human life ought to be about. In doing so he highlighted two aspects which he said formed a summary, not only of his own teaching recorded in the New Testament, but also of the whole of the Old Testament (the first four-fifths of the Bible). This means that the whole Bible in all its vastness is in complete agreement on this summary of human beings' two-fold duty:

> "And [Jesus] said [to a lawyer who questioned him], 'You shall love the Lord your God with all your heart and with all your soul and with all your mind. This is the great and first commandment. And a second is like it: You shall love your neighbour as yourself. On these two commandments depend all the law and the prophets.'"
> (Matthew 22:37-40)

Two things, then, define our responsibilities if we want to live a life which is in harmony with what God envisaged for us and if we want to build something truly fulfilling. The first responsibility is to love God; the second is to love our neighbour, in other words, our fellow man and woman. This would include family and friends, neighbours, colleagues, casual acquaintances, strangers we randomly come across and perhaps even mankind at large. In fact, it even includes our enemies, a feature with further singles out the uniqueness of Jesus' message. Notice that, alarmingly, there is nothing here about loving ourselves! Jesus probably knew that we would do this anyway without having to be told – it's virtually an instinct. But we definitely *do* have to be told to put God in first place, and we *do* have to be reminded about our responsibilities to our fellow human beings. To try to do these things is the great secret of life.

There is something wonderfully selfless and recognisably right in what Jesus is saying here. It is at once devastatingly simple yet incredibly hard to carry out – a true lifelong challenge (particularly the part about loving one's enemies). But it is a challenge more worthwhile than any other. Jesus invites us to look outside ourselves and our own little cocoon of a world dominated by self in order to focus instead upon God and upon helping others. If we do this we will, in our own small way, be giving glory to God and taking up our part in fulfilling His prime directive.

Not an option

We should pause a moment to consider the rationale for Jesus' two-pronged command. It's perhaps clear enough why Jesus would have asked us to show love to our fellow man and woman. The benefits for society and the human race at large are obvious and Jesus' words correspondingly find their counterpart in a number of ethical systems and religious traditions in the world. Many people, whether or not they believe in God, would nod and acquiesce to this principle, recognising that if only people were more willing to do this the world would be a much better place in which to live. Focusing on relationships with others is definitely a better place to be than amassing stuff and experiences focused primarily on entertaining ourselves.

Such people might be much less comfortable with the other half of Jesus' command however: the part about loving God and putting Him first. Showing love and consideration towards our fellow humans is all very well and indeed to be commended, they might say, but surely we can do without all this God business? Couldn't we have the moral code and brotherly spirit of helping our fellow man and woman without the need for the religious dimension?

While this might be a tempting option, particularly for those who find little inclination towards organised religion, it would mean becoming only half the person we are meant to be. When we talk about our first responsibility being to centre our lives on God it's not really about our personal views of religious culture and habit (those are finer points that can be debated later). Instead, we're dealing with a more fundamental question of what it means to be a human being. What the Bible is effectively saying is that we were designed for worship, to be focused on another rather than primarily on ourselves. We are built to seek for something more, something *higher*, something *better* than ourselves. This something – this mind of which our minds are but imperfect impressions – is God, and we will only truly be all we are meant to be as persons when we find ourselves in Him. That God-shaped hole in our hearts can only be filled when we live in relation to Him and find completion there.

To live any other way is, in a sense, a form of idolatry in which we worship an imaginary false 'god' – a god that doesn't really exist. We are meant to worship the true God: the Supernatural power within the universe, the Creator, the great Mind behind it all who brought everything into being. If, instead, we make the focus of our lives our own ambition, our career, the pursuit of material things or pleasure, even other people – *anything*, in fact, other than the God we were designed to seek, then we end up focusing upon and worshipping *created things* rather than the Creator of those things. That cannot possibly be right; the Creator must be more important and ultimately more worthy than what He has created. If we make the mistake of ignoring Him we miss the point of life and find ourselves dissatisfied.

Thus Jesus insists that both of these two elements are essential: to love God and to love our neighbour. It is not an either-or choice he is presenting us with. Instead we must attempt to fulfil both aspects as our highest calling and our greatest good.

Chapter 11

Something's not right

SO there is a point – a reason – behind both our own existence as individuals and behind the wider world as an expression of God's creative genius. So far so good; all this sounds very fine and it would be wonderful if we could conclude the book at this point by saying 'and they all lived happily ever after'. But of course it isn't as simple as that. This is only the pleasant half of the story – that which *ought* to be, when in fact it very plainly *isn't*.

Contradiction

When we look at the world around us we find there is a shocking contradiction. On the one had there is stunning evidence of beauty, design and orchestration in the world, the sense that it is all 'meant to be', utterly wonderful in its conception and execution. Think of the splendour of a clear starry night, the burbles of a contented newborn, the smell of a walk through a forest after rain, the artistry in the snow and ice on a frosty morning, the joy of companionship with good friends. We might well experience these and a myriad other aspects of life and see them as reflecting the character and glory of a good God carrying out His purpose much as the prime directive would lead us to expect. All these examples seem to chime nicely with God's objective of filling the world with His glory.

But it's not by any means a complete picture of what our world is like. The camera pans now and we see a country ripped apart by civil war, and the millions of tons of waste and landfill that are produced every year. Again the camera pans and we see the ongoing problem of the abuse of women and children; we witness families starving and struggling from poor sanitation. What has gone wrong? How do these things show the glory of God? How do they even belong in the same world? If God wants the world to be full of His glory and hence free of injustice and exploitation, then why isn't it?

Are we there yet?

The world we are in now is very clearly *not* the world full of God's glory that He finally envisages and there are a couple of possibilities why this might be so. One is that God has somehow made a mistake and can't quite get His plan to work out properly; intuitively this feels rather unlikely given His obvious success as a creator. Another possibility is that the world as we see it today is not the world as it is meant to be – we have simply not yet arrived at our final destination.

It is this latter possibility which is the right answer. Today's world is not the final goal but rather an intermediary step, a bridge or stepping-stone on the way to the world God ultimately wants. It might help to think of a building site as an analogy. A building site is, let's face it, a pretty unattractive thing. There are cranes and scaffolding everywhere, huge piles of sand and cement, rubbish skips, disrupted traffic, barricades – we all know the scene (and the mess that goes with it). No one would design a building site as the end goal of a project.

But the intriguing thing about a building site is the *potential* it contains – the thought of what it will be after the work and mess is done. A building site represents a project underway but not completed – but one day everything will be different and a building that is both splendid and genuinely useful will hopefully be revealed. Architects don't design building sites, they design buildings. But buildings don't make themselves and if you want to reach the end goal of the beautiful building, wonderfully appointed and magnificent to look at, then first of all you must have the building site. The end justifies the means.

God's building site

Looking at the problems and inadequacies of the current world and concluding that God isn't a very good designer or that He doesn't exist at all is a bit like looking at the building site and assuming it is the end-game, the final result that God as the great architect has planned. No one would criticise a regular architect because of the state of a building site, but unfortunately people do this all the time when it comes to God. God's end goal is most emphatically not the world as we see it today any more than a building site is the final intention of an architect. It is a huge mistake to judge God's great plan for the earth by the state of the world as we currently find it.

But is it really true that we have to pass through the building site stage and have all the problems and inadequacies in order to ultimately fulfil the prime directive of a world full of God's glory? If God wanted such a world, why didn't He simply create it like that in the first place? The answer to this lies in the idea of free choice.

Chapter 12

Under construction

TRAGIC but true, most of the problems which spoil the world today are ultimately caused by human choice. It is human beings who choose to go to war, who vie for power and control over others, who exploit one another, engage in corruption and cronyism, and who fail to equally distribute the planet's resources. It is human beings who abuse one another, who steal and commit crimes, who say cruel things and envy one another. The essential *cause* for the paradox of the oh-so-good-yet-oh-so-bad world we live in seems to lie predominantly with *us* as human beings.

This clash of good and evil has been endlessly captured in literature and film (think *Lord of the Rings* or *Star Wars* to name just two, but they are the tip of the iceberg). It is a theme of which we seem never to tire as a race, but why? Why should we be so fascinated by this dichotomy, this endless battle between good and evil told time and time again in so many different variants and through so many media? Perhaps it is because as individuals we are all caught up in that very drama which we recognise is at play in the world. We know the struggle is there – perhaps even within our own selves – and so we reflect on the conflict again and again with inescapable fascination. At heart we know that it is not a battle of Sith versus Jedi or Mordor versus Shire but rather a battle which Is all together more personal. It is the human dilemma – a drama which has the paradox of human nature at its core.

The harsh reality

We need to dig further into this. One of the defining factors of being human is our conscience and our ability to make free choices. According to the Bible we have this very special ability which rises above mere instinct and Pavlovian response because God has given it to us as one of His most precious yet costly gifts, one which so distinguishes us from the animals.

Why did He do this when one of the consequences is the presence of so much suffering and evil? Perhaps there are two closely related ways of answering this, one positive and one negative.

To the negative, the alternative would be for us to be mere robots running on pre-programmed code or lesser animals governed by instincts we could never rise above. Is that really what either He or we would want? Alternatively He could allow us to choose good but then electrocute us when we choose bad – but this is not freedom! This is the world of Pavlov's dogs, of lab-rats trained with treats and shocks. God would have made us so much less if He had not made us truly free and allowed us to genuinely face the consequences of our actions.

To the positive, the gift of freewill allows the creation of something of true value and character, the possibility of our growing to become more than what we were before. It is free will that creates the potential for real love, for true compassion and forgiveness and for relationships which exist not because they have to, but because we choose to commit to them wherever it may take us. It is free choice that unlocks the possibility for deep relationships and true fellowship not just with each other but with God Himself.

At the end of the day the price of human freedom is a high one, but it is a price God rightly considered worth paying. God does not get any satisfaction or enjoyment out of those occasions when we make bad choices and suffer the consequences as we must; no, it upsets and hurts Him just as it would a parent when they see their child make unwise decisions. On the other hand, He loves it when we choose of our own free will to seek and worship Him, when we show that we value what He has said by trying to put it into practice, and when we engage with Him in meditation, fellowship and prayer. When things do go wrong He is always on hand to welcome us back with open arms and to provide direction for the future just as a human parent would.

He wants to save us, but He will not force His love upon us. The quality of our relationship with Him is therefore down to our choosing.

The big picture

The big picture, when we step back and consider things from the level of human society at large, is as follows. Man's greatest service and greatest honour is to worship God by doing what God wants (that is the best that worship can be – freely and willingly given). But God will not force this upon us; it is down to us to make a choice. Often human beings have chosen to centre their world on themselves rather than God and at times they have done this in highly unscrupulous ways. That's the cause of the exploitation, the mis-distribution, the mismanagement. It's the inevitable consequence of free will. We must be very careful not to blame God for choices that we as a race have made. Would we really want Him to reduce us to lower animals or robots so that the bad choices of the past would not have happened? No, the power of choice contains within it the potential for good of such magnitude and relationships of such beauty that we surely would not wish it away. But we must be prepared to stomach the consequences and understand that in some measure we are each implicated in them.

It is human free will, therefore, that creates this 'building site' period that we are in – a world on the way to becoming the one which God wants, but a world which has definitely not yet arrived at its final destination. We can be confident, however, that all the trials and tribulations of the construction process will be well worth it in the end. God promises it. If He can be trusted to fashion the stars and the planets, to create the seas and the forests, and the infinity of incredible creatures that inhabit them, if He can enable music and art, companionship and humour, then He can be trusted to know what He is talking about when He tells us of His great plans for the world in all their wonder. As Jesus puts it:

"If you then, who are evil" (i.e., if you, as sinners who sometimes lie, cheat and oppress), "know how to give good gifts to your children, how much more will your Father who is in heaven give good things to those who ask him!" (Matthew 7:11)

Chapter 13

The human conundrum

AT the heart of all human beings there is an astonishing paradox. How can it be that as a species we can be capable of such wonderful acts of self-sacrifice and yet at the same time acts of unspeakable cruelty? How can it be that there can be a Hitler and a Mother Teresa both made out of the same stuff? Even more bizarre, how can *the same person* one minute show such love and caring attention in one situation, and in the next moment turn around and be curt, cruel or even victimise or torture others? What *is* this paradox that lies at the heart of our nature?

The dark side

The Bible says that in the beginning men and women were made in the image of God, something which is not said about any of the other animals. This probably refers to our unique human attributes of personhood: our intellectual, emotional, linguistic, aesthetic and relational capabilities. We are well aware of the good things humans are capable of: many of us experience virtues like love, patience, forgiveness and self-sacrifice shown to us by others on a daily basis, and we probably try to show them ourselves as far as we can.

But we also need to recognise the other side, unpleasant though it may be, because we need an account for that too. All is not sweetness and light as far as human beings are concerned. We take the good stuff for granted, but we also need an account of human evil to explain statistics like the following:

- More than 26,000 children die each day because of poverty, yet there are enough resources on the planet to go round. Why haven't we sorted this out by now?

- There are around 640 million firearms in the world – one for every ten people. Why? Can't we trust one another enough without carrying weapons so that we can use them on someone if they happen to transgress or get on our bad side?
- Around one in three women are physically or sexually abused during their lives.
- One to two million children are sexually exploited every year.
- At any time there are typically more than thirty violent political conflicts and wars underway in the world.

Surely we must have an account for this, an understanding of how such things can be and whether anything can be done about it? It is simply too large an issue to sweep under the carpet and it's one that isn't going away.

Possible explanations

People have grappled with this question for millennia. Many argued that we are the victims of an epic cosmic battle being waged around us: caught, as it were, in the crossfire of spiritual and demonic powers which we can only hope to influence through mysterious rituals. In ancient Persia people thought that there were two basic forces of good and evil locked in eternal combat. All misfortune and trouble in the world was put down to the impact of this cosmic struggle. But none of this fits with what we have already seen about the superior power and wisdom of God as creator and reason for everything. If He is as great as both the Bible and creation demand then it makes no sense to picture Him locked in constant battle in which He vies for supremacy with His nemesis or some demonic supernatural force. This sort of 'cosmic battle' explanation simply won't work.

Today another view is popular: that evil is no more than social evolution not yet having run its full course. Through evolutionary and sociological processes , we are told, society is gradually improving and the world is getting better. Just as creatures evolved over time (it is said), so, too, society is evolving and finding better ways of organizing and structuring itself. As this happens problems of the kind we've listed will increasingly become things of the past.

It's a popular view, but is it true? Is it credible to think that society is gradually getting better, and that it can fix its own problems? Let's run a few tests to see.

- How are we doing with resolving geopolitical tensions? Are there fewer wars or potential wars today than in the past? In the last 150 years alone we've seen two world wars, the Holocaust, the ethnic cleansing of the Balkans and of Cambodia, the pogroms, and the purges of Mao, to name just a few examples.
- Is the world a safer place than it has been, on a national or local scale? Do we need more or less security?
- Do we find better, more stable and enduring family relationships or are we gradually witnessing the fragmentation and atomization of society?
- Are there any fewer natural or ecological disasters?
- Are politicians any more trustworthy? Are they any more likely to solve society's problems?
- When we read the newspaper or browse the internet news, is it any more cheery and hopeful than it would have been, say, ten years ago – or twenty, or fifty?

This is not to imply that *nothing* good has been done in the world, that there have been no positive changes in society, or that human beings are incapable of doing good and kind things. Far from it. There have been all kinds of programs and initiatives which have helped communities and nations immensely – we keep trying to make things better, and it is right that we do so. But the world as a whole is still in a mess and, in some respects, in a *worse* mess than ever before. Why?

The Bible's explanation for the troubles in the world is very simple, and, for many, much more compelling than what sociologists, scientists, anthropologists or philosophers have to offer. The problem starts, not with cosmic battles or the shortcomings of past evolutionary states, but instead much nearer home: with *us* – with what we essentially are as human beings, and with something called *sin*.

Chapter 14

The 'S' word

A S concepts go, the idea of 'sin' is, frankly speaking, pretty unpopular. The very mention of it creates an instinctive negative reaction. Who wants to hear criticism of themselves? Is there really any need to be so negative and to condemn everyone in such a sweeping way? The idea of sin – the very word – may also call to mind institutions like confession with all the negative feelings of guilt that have been inculcated.

But none of these are reasons for not taking seriously the reality and ramifications of sin. The fact that sin is an unpleasant concept says nothing about whether or not it is true. If we are to face the truth about the world we live in and some of the appalling statistics we looked at in the last chapter, then we really must start by being honest about ourselves.

Self, God, and others

So, what is sin, and how does it help us understand the dark side of our world?

The Bible explains it simply: sin is what happens when we do what *we* want to do rather than what God wants us to do. It's about putting self before God and others. It's a somewhat trite point, but one that bears repeating: the word sin has the word 'I' tucked away there right in the middle of it ('s-I-n'). That is the fundamental problem of sin: it puts *me* first when that's the place that ought to be held only by God.

One of the Hebrew words that the Bible uses for the concept (it has several!) has the literal meaning of 'to miss the target'. This is another helpful metaphor to understand sin. It implies that God has set the standard or the target behaviour human beings should be striving for: the keeping of His commands and the doing of His will. When we fall short of this by doing our own thing and disobeying Him ('missing the target'), then we sin.

All kinds of consequences flow from this simple notion of sin as a rejection of God's commands in favour of self. From sin comes anger, greed, hatred, murder, exploitation, theft, vandalism, adultery, broken homes, disrespect, war, envy, terrorism ... the list goes on and on. Sin explains why human society is in the state it is. It explains the origin of the environmental crisis, unsafe neighbourhoods, racial tension, sexual abuse, unfair distribution of wealth, domestic violence – virtually all the evils the world forces us to face every time we turn on the TV or listen to the news.

But it does more than that. It also explains what goes on in our own personal lives and in our own hearts every day. We all have a sense of what we would *like* to be – an ideal, if you like – as a father or mother, a husband or wife, a neighbour, an employee, a friend, or simply as a human being. But we rarely seem to be able to quite achieve it. We come home from work and we're tired, so we might be short-tempered with our partner or push the children away instead of being patient with them when they want to show us something they've done. We might argue or be unpleasant with someone just because we feel like it. We might be glad about someone else's misfortune if it helps us get ahead. None of these is the way we would ideally want to behave, perhaps, yet time and again we seem to fall short of the potential to get it right. This 'sin' isn't just something that's 'out there' that we can pin on others whom we label 'criminals'; it's in each one of us as individuals too.

Joining the dots

It is an essential step to connect the experience of inadequacy and sin in our own personal lives with the problems that exist in the world at large in this way. The two are intrinsically related – crucially and inevitably – for it's the same basic problem that lies at the heart of both: the problem of missing the target, of self over God. We shouldn't just sit like some tabloid journalist wagging a finger at others or at society's problems as if we didn't have a hand in them.

We may think that the examples in our own lives are relatively inconsequential in comparison to some of the atrocities in the world at large (this is the 'but I've never murdered anyone!' defence), and it will very probably be true that there is a significant difference of scale or degree. But the point we mustn't lose sight of is that the basic process that has taken place in our own personal experience is the one we see played out time and time again in society at large.

The famous bygone writer G. K. Chesterton was once asked by a major national newspaper to write a letter stating what he believed to be wrong with the universe. His letter was very brief:

> Dear Sirs,
>
> I am.

It was a very perceptive answer. There was no finger pointing here, except at himself. He had appreciated the very point that Jesus had made many centuries before when he said:

> "From within, out of the heart of man, come evil thoughts, sexual immorality, theft, murder, adultery, coveting, wickedness, deceit, sensuality, envy, slander, pride, foolishness. All these evil things come from within, and they defile a person." (Mark 7:21-23)

Hundreds of years before that a prophet by the name of Jeremiah similarly exclaimed:

> "The heart is deceitful above all things, and desperately sick; who can understand it?"   (Jeremiah 17:9)

This is not to say that we don't ever do anything good or that there is not the capacity for selfless giving in human beings – clearly there is, and we see numerous examples of it. But it is not all sweetness and light by any means. When you think of some of the terrible acts of cruelty and oppression that have taken place in human history and that are still unfolding today, it's hard not to agree with these assessments from the Bible and to be ashamed of ourselves as a race. Although humans do many, many good things, there is a whole lot of bad that needs to be explained and remedied.

The problem, then, is not some epic cosmic battle involving someone or something else – the problem is instead one which relates to each of us as human beings at a very personal level, and which thus affects all humanity. Society's problems are problems which arise because of what *we are* as human beings. Human hearts, human nature and sin are the problem which needs to be addressed, and that's something that starts within the heart of each one of us. We can't really start to find the solution unless we first take responsibility for our own behaviour and own the problem at the personal level.

Chapter 15

A brief history of sin

THE first book of the Bible is the book of Genesis. The word 'Genesis' means 'beginning' – and that is indeed what the book of Genesis is: a great place to start in understanding both the great truths about God and the truth about ourselves. In the Bible's view, you'll remember, everything begins with God – it's about Him before it's about us. In its first two chapters Genesis describes how God creates the earth and man and woman, makes a special home for them (the Garden of Eden), gives them a responsible and rewarding job to do, and permits them to eat of any tree within the garden except the one tree in the centre, the tree of knowledge of good and evil.

By doing this God is giving the man and the woman a fulfilling purpose, enabling them to enjoy the wonderful environment He has put them in virtually to the full. They are also invited to have a close personal relationship with their Maker in a world in which they have everything they need to be happy and fulfilled. Everything seems wonderful, and that's how it is when you start with God.

Boundaries

But a standard of behaviour was required. There was a boundary, a condition. God has given humans free will, not made them robots. He wants to see them actively choose to do what He asks not because they are forced to but because they *want* to and because they think it is *right*. He wants the love, trust and obedience of beings willingly given. But this gift of free will brings with it consequences. What if we choose to reject Him? What if we question His boundaries and terms, or even flatly ignore them? Bound up in the possibility of a free choice to love and serve God must be the possibility of rejecting Him.

And that is exactly what happened in the beginning with Adam and Eve. The choice of disobedience that Adam and Eve made by taking the forbidden fruit was not only a choice of putting themselves first (despite the negative consequences God told them it would have), it was also the assertion that they knew better than God what was good for them. It was the first sin.

As an account of our nature this is tremendously powerful. It means that from the very beginning (we are only two or three pages into the Bible at this point) we have an account of where all the problems of humanity come from and a ready ability to understand not only the good but also the potential of evil within us. It doesn't stretch the bounds of credibility at all to claim that most of the world's problems are the result of human choice and selfishness. It clearly makes sense. Yet surprisingly, many of the world's religions do not have a doctrine that really explains and tackles sin. They are not able to explain in a convincing way, therefore, either the human conundrum or why the world needs fixing. Consequently, they struggle to present a solution, which means that they fail to provide a real source of hope. One of the most powerful things about the Bible is that it presents both the central problem of our existence and an explanation of it right at the very start. The Bible stares the world straight in the eye and tells it like it is. Once that has been done, then we can start to think about the sort of solution we might need.

Consequences

It is absurd, when you stop to think about it, that Adam and Eve should have made the choice they did – and indeed, all sin is absurd from this perspective. It just makes no sense, even though we do it all the time. How could we possibly know better than God what is right and good for us when He made us in the first place? He wrote the rule-book, after all; He made us and is bound to know what's best! Adam and Eve's sin was a rejection of God and His boundaries, a denial of the fact that God knows best. It is sin in all the ways we've considered it in the last chapter – both a missing of the target behaviour and a putting of self before Him. This is how sin came into the world and how the sad story of a world still under construction began – a world struggling under the burden of sin and suffering.

The problem with breaking God's commands as Adam and Eve decided to do is that there are repercussions. Though Adam tried to blame Eve and Eve tried to blame the serpent, God insisted that they each took responsibility as adults for what they had done. God tells us about right and wrong for our own good, and He had made it very clear to Adam and Eve what the implications of disobeying Him would be. Despite that, they chose to do their own thing – so what was God to do? Say, 'Well, that's OK. Never mind about my instruction. It wasn't really that important anyway ...'? That would make a mockery of Him saying they shouldn't have done it in the first place.

If you think about it, there have to be consequences for human sin. If God's standards are at all important and are the basis on which the whole universe operates properly to its maximum potential, then He has to *make* them important. Imagine you are a parent and you tell your child it's important to behave in a certain way. If the child then does the opposite and you do nothing whatsoever about it then your parenting will not be very successful and your child will probably not grow up to be very pleasant.

The consequence of Adam and Eve's disobedience was that suffering and death came into the world. At the end of the day this is why we die – because of sin. If we didn't the world would end up being populated by immortal sinners which would be massively counter-productive to God's plans for a great world. Instead, even man's environment became cursed and unstable, rebelling against him, as it were, as he tried to exercise his dominion over it – just as he had rebelled against God. Now Adam's responsibilities became a hardship and a struggle for him: from now on he was to work with sweat, suffering and hard graft to eat food until at last he would fall to the ground dead. God was teaching Adam and Eve – and all who read their story – that there is a consequence to our actions. And while these consequences might at first sound extreme (since they ultimately included death), if God had not imposed a limit on human life then He would effectively have been permitting them to go on disobeying Him and living contrary to the great principles of reality forever![1] Hardly an acceptable state of affairs.

Escalation

Can it get any worse? Oh yes, it can! You would think that having seen the consequences of their mistake, the humans would have addressed the problem and put it behind them once and for all. But the problem of sin didn't stop with Adam and Eve. All human beings have inherited the legacy of Adam and Eve's sin since they are descended from them and inherit the same basic nature. Like our forebears, we too have a necessarily mortal existence subject to pain and suffering, naturally estranged from God and inclined to put our own interests forward more often than we should. In big things and small human beings today follow the same pattern of challenging God's boundaries, thinking that they know better than He, and putting their wants ahead of His. Then they find someone else to blame or make excuses for themselves when things go wrong; we live in a culture of blame, yet somehow it's never *us* who are the ones who are at fault!

One of the fascinating and frightening truths taught by these early chapters of Genesis is that the pattern of sin which Adam and Eve began does not just repeat itself, it actually gets worse. One might think that taking a piece of forbidden fruit is a triviality. But in the very next chapter after the Fall, the Bible records the first account of family life. In it, Adam's first son Cain is so jealous and resentful of his brother Abel that he murders him and thus the first of the myriad

---

1   Since we are all sinners, this would imply a world of immortal sinners. Why should God allow that when our sin offends Him and when it is so *wrong*? If human beings choose to break God's commands and go against the fundamental principles of the universe it is only right that their lives should come to an end, especially given the fact their lives are a gift from Him in the first place.

murders of human history is committed. The very first family the world has known was thus completely dysfunctional and torn apart by murder. This powerfully illustrates the potential of where human nature can quickly lead. The Bible tells it like it is: a warts-and-all account of what human selfishness accomplishes if left unchecked. As the early chapters of Genesis prove, the problem of little sins is that they quickly beget big ones. This is why sin is serious and why we need God's help.

The point is this – sin escalates. It does not solve itself or quietly go away. If it is unchecked, it gets worse and worse. The first eleven chapters of Genesis, right at the beginning of the Bible, describe a degeneration of society, a downward spiral as men and women move further and further away from God. One act of violence or rebellion leads to another which is worse, and that new act of sin is topped yet again. It repeats and repeats down the generations impacting every human being who has ever lived.

Temptation

So how does it happen?

At the end of the day sin impacts us all. We make wrong choices ourselves and we inherit the consequences not only of our own mistakes but of the sins of others as well, whether they are the sins of individuals, groups or institutions. James, one of the early followers of Jesus, describes how this happens and what the consequences are:

"Each person is tempted when he is lured and enticed by his own desire. Then desire when it has conceived gives birth to sin, and sin when it is fully grown brings forth death." (James 1:14,15)

Notice that James makes this personal – 'each person'. It's not about pointing the finger at society or at others – whether it's other nations, other races, other neighbourhoods, political leaders, one's parents, social background, educators, or who- or what-ever else. Nor is it about pointing the finger at some group over there who we label 'criminals'. All of those groups may be blameworthy in very real ways, but the place to start for each of us is right at home with what we need to change in ourselves. It's about seeing that there is a fundamental problem with human beings at large, but that each of us struggles with the same essential issue on an individual basis. It's the same basic problem wherever we look in the world. The problem is sin, and if only we can own the problem then we can turn to God for help in trying to find our way back to Him again.

Chapter 16

Eureka!

ACCORDING to legend, when Archimedes the great Greek engineer and inventor came up with his idea of how to raise water from one level to another using a screw, he happened to be in the bath. So excited was he about his new invention that he jumped out crying 'Eureka!' (the Greek way of saying 'I've found it!') and ran out of the house and down the street stark naked to tell everyone about it.

While such an action is not to be recommended in the modern world, the fact remains that finding the answer to an incredibly important problem can be both exhilarating and life-changing. This chapter introduces God's solution to the biggest systemic problem humans have ever had to deal with yet often fail to recognise: the problem of human nature and its consequences.

Two sets of problems

When we think about the implications and consequences of the bad side of human nature, there are basically two issues that need to be addressed: problems in the world at large (wars, exploitation, imperfect justice and penal systems, abuse, etc.), and the failings of human beings as individuals. Let's take a closer look at each of these.

First, there are 'universal' or worldwide problems which seem just too huge and insurmountable for mankind to effectively handle on any kind of permanent or comprehensive basis: things like wars (let's say, for instance, the Middle East conflict), hunger, natural disasters, disease, the aging epidemic, climate change, terrorism, exploitation, the gulf between the 'haves' and the 'have-nots'. For most of us these may not necessarily affect us personally (if we're lucky enough to be one of the 'haves'), but that doesn't mean these issues are not real or serious. We need a hope that one day the world will be better than this, that a solution to these enormous difficulties will be found and that society will be able to function in a more wholesome way. First, then, we have universal, society-wide problems.

Second, there are more personal issues. We argued earlier that society's problems as a whole can be traced back to a fundamental problem within each one of us – the problem of selfishness and sin. This means that when we think about our own lives we have the issue of our own personal inadequacies, whatever they might be: things like anger, impatience, laziness, unkindness, destructive choices, or greed. We need to hope that those flaws and inadequacies that we each possess can be dealt with also – that we can be forgiven, that we can find purpose and meaning in spite of them, and that the burdens we each carry can be taken away – in short, that we can become more than we currently are.

The good news

The good news, momentous in its impact and far more exciting than Archimedes' brainwave, is that God has a specific plan to address both of these types of problem. But exactly what *is* that solution which unlocks God's great plans for the world? On the one hand, how can He help with the global problems like war, inequality and starvation – and will He? If the world is indeed riddled with human-derived problems, then what is God's plan to address and solve them? And on the other hand, how can He help *you* in *your* life with *your* own inadequacies, fears and weaknesses – or *me* in *mine*? How can we become better and more fulfilled and hopeful people because of what He has done?

In essence what we have to do is stop relying on ourselves to make things better, stop blaming other people and other things, and start relying on God rather than ignoring Him. Human beings don't *have* to go it alone. God offers both help and hope. He has a specific, definite and decisive plan; a plan that can give us a true and transforming hope.

Two solutions

The solution finds its centre in the work of God's Son the Lord Jesus Christ. You see, we might think that it is the large scale problems – the society-wide ones – which are the real issues. But actually it is the other way round. It is the common human nature that we all share and the problem of the sins we each commit as individuals (whether they be large or small) which is the bigger, more systemic problem. It is individual selfishness and the corruptible nature that we each bear which, when scaled up across peoples and societies, gives rise to the larger scale problems. Address the problem of sin at the individual level, therefore, and you have the potential and the hope of one day solving it at the worldwide level.

Jesus' first work, therefore (we're thinking now about when he was first here on the earth about two thousand years ago) was to deal with the issue of individual sin. He did so powerfully and effectively through both his teaching and his perfect behaviour, and then by decisively offering his life as both a sacrifice and an example for us.

But that is not the end of the story; it's only the first half of the solution in fact. God also promises to send Jesus back to the earth a second time to deal with the worldwide problems (the so-called 'Second Coming'). God promises that one day the earth will be filled with His glory: that it will be free of injustice, inadequacy, and all evil so that His prime directive can finally be accomplished. He promises this very solemnly and specifically not just once but on three separate occasions in the Bible (we looked at this in chapter 9, page 31). Many, many more times the Bible speaks of God's future kingdom on earth in which Jesus will be king – a time when there will at last be true peace and justice in the world. Clearly, Jesus isn't here yet. This promise has not yet been fulfilled, which is why the world is as we see it today: so imperfect for all it promises so much. This promise of God remains to be fulfilled in the future. It is the future hope which the Bible offers and it will be the answer to our biggest questions.

Chapter 17

The 'Good News' headlines

AFTER Jesus had died and rose again, his apostles and followers began the work of preaching the Gospel message throughout the world. Some of the significant milestones of that work are recorded in a Bible book called 'The Acts of the Apostles' (or simply 'Acts' for short). It describes the rapid growth of Christianity as it spread like wildfire throughout the Roman Empire about two thousand years ago.

The teaching of the apostles

One of the interesting things about Acts is that it contains several summaries of the good news that the apostles originally taught – the very heart of what the Gospel message is all about. These summaries are very useful in ensuring that we're on the right track in understanding the true message of Bible hope. Unfortunately, in later times a number of pagan ideas and philosophies were brought into the church and mixed with the original truth, but by going back to Acts and other places in the New Testament we can determine the essence of the Gospel that Jesus and the apostles believed.

Here, then, are a few of those summaries of that Gospel message:

"When they believed [the Apostle] Philip as he preached good news about **the kingdom of God** and **the name of Jesus Christ**, they were baptized, both men and women."   (Acts 8:12)

"From morning till evening [the Apostle Paul] expounded to them, testifying to **the kingdom of God**, and trying to convince them **about Jesus** both from the Law of Moses and from the Prophets."   (Acts 28:23)

"[Paul] lived there two whole years at his own expense, and welcomed all who came to him, proclaiming **the kingdom of God** and teaching about **the Lord Jesus Christ** with all boldness and without hindrance." (Acts 28:30,31)

You probably spotted the pattern. In each of these passages there are two key elements:

1. The things concerning the kingdom of God;
2. The name of Jesus Christ.

These two aspects – the kingdom of God and Jesus Christ – provide a kind of short-hand summary of God's answer to human problems; they are, in essence, what the Bible's message is all about.

The teaching of Jesus

We can corroborate this evidence from the book of Acts and confirm that we're on the right track in focusing on these two aspects by looking at some events in Jesus' own life. In the Christmas narrative the angel Gabriel appears to Mary to announce that she will have a child. It's fascinating to notice that Gabriel speaks about exactly these same two topics that we just found in Acts:

"And the angel said to [Mary], 'Do not be afraid, Mary, for you have found favour with God. And behold, you will conceive in your womb and bear a son, and you shall **call his name Jesus**. He will be great and will be **called the Son of the Most High**. And the Lord God will give to him **the throne** of his father David, and **he will reign** over the house of Jacob forever, and of **his kingdom** there will be no end." (Luke 1:30-33)

Notice that the angel talks about:

1. Jesus' name and identity (the name of Jesus Christ).
2. His future role as king over God's everlasting kingdom (the things concerning the kingdom of God).

We are finding an interesting thread here. If we were to continue through the Gospels to look at Jesus' teaching we would find that a great deal of what Jesus had to say could be classified under those two subjects: *himself* (as Saviour and God's unique messenger), and *the kingdom*.[1] Here are just a few examples of each:

Jesus' teaching about himself:

"Jesus said to him, '**I** am the way, and the truth, and the life. No one comes to the Father except through **me**.'" (John 14:6)

"**I** am the door. If anyone enters by **me**, he will be saved ..." (John 10:9)

"Again Jesus spoke to them, saying, '**I** am the light of the world. Whoever follows **me** will not walk in darkness, but will have the light of life.'" (John 8:12)

Jesus' teaching about the kingdom:

"Now after John was arrested, Jesus came into Galilee, proclaiming the gospel of God, and saying, 'The time is fulfilled, and **the kingdom of God** is at hand; repent and believe in the gospel.'" (Mark 1:14,15)

"He presented himself alive to them after his suffering by many proofs, appearing to them during forty days and speaking about **the kingdom of God**." (Acts 1:3)

Two problems, two solutions

The evidence is pretty compelling: the Gospel message in the New Testament focuses on the kingdom of God and on the name and work of the Lord Jesus Christ. Quite clearly, understanding these two components is absolutely fundamental to a proper grasp of Bible teaching. But why these two aspects in particular?

---

1 He also had a huge amount to say about what sort of people we should try to be and what sort of lives we should lead in order to have a relationship with him and to prepare for the kingdom; we shall look briefly at that towards the end of this book.

Chapter 18

The golden thread

ONE powerful answer to the question why the New Testament focuses so much on the twin topics of Jesus and the kingdom of God is that they match up precisely with the two types of human need ('the problem') that we've been considering in earlier chapters. We noted that for all the 'big picture' problems in society at large there is a more fundamental and systemic problem that impacts us all – the problem of human nature, sin and selfishness. It is precisely this that is dealt with and remedied by the great work Jesus accomplished the first time he was upon the earth. Christ's death as a sacrifice for sins creates the potential solution to the systemic problem of sin and it enables each of us as individuals to come back into a good relationship with God. If we understand the things concerning the name of Jesus Christ, his life and his work, then we shall come face to face with God's solution to our greatest need as individuals. We shall be focusing on this in the next few chapters.

How will we get there?

But what about society at large? It's all very well for you or me to have the potential for a good relationship with God through the work of Jesus, but what about those society-wide problems like pollution, wars, exploitation, social tensions, abuse, crime, sickness and disease and the like? How will they be solved – and when?

Thinking abstractly about it, there are several *theoretically possible* answers as to how such a solution might be achieved, but only one of them in fact represents the truth. It could be, for instance, that God is going to take His followers away from the earth and enable them to have a better existence somewhere else – but this is quite definitely *not* the message of the Bible. Alternatively, it could be (we might suppose) that society will gradually improve itself with God's help: it will become more cultured, more sophisticated and more spiritual; we will gradually solve more and more of these issues until the earth is finally transformed into the sort of place that God originally intended. But this is not the teaching of the Bible either.

No, the Bible offers neither of those hopes. Instead, it states very clearly that in the future God will set up His kingdom right here on the earth in which these global issues will finally be resolved. This has always been His plan, and He will carry it out as He has repeatedly promised during the hundreds of years in which the Bible was written. It will take place when He sends Jesus back again to the earth (the 'Second Coming') to be the world's future king. This, then, is the second of the two crucial elements of God's message in the Bible – the things concerning the kingdom of God.

A much bigger story

These twin elements about Jesus and the kingdom are also found throughout the Old Testament, so that the whole Bible is united by these themes. Right at the very beginning, at the very moment when Adam and Eve first sinned, God spoke of His plan for the future: that one day a special descendent would come who would fight against sin and death and conquer them once and for all. Later on God made great promises to a man called Abraham (the father of both Jewish and Arab peoples) which spoke of the future kingdom of God and the coming of the Lord Jesus, who would be Abraham's descendent. To Moses (the one who brought Israel out of slavery in Egypt and gave them the Ten Commandments) God spoke again of a future prophet who would be like him and yet far greater (once again, He was speaking of Jesus). So too to David, the archetypal Old Testament king, and to the prophets like Isaiah and Daniel, God spoke both about the future kingdom and about the Lord Jesus Christ who would one day be sent by God.

It is no exaggeration to say that the whole Bible is filled with God's promises – they form a rhythmic pulse which drives the whole thing forward, on and on towards the great future that God is planning for the world. The promises of God are consistent, grounded in infinite wisdom and understanding, and they are repeated like an insistent drumbeat which underpins the whole Bible. God's great solution is something that was promised hundreds and thousands of years before and has always been part of His grand design.

The golden thread

It becomes apparent, then, that God didn't gradually came to the conclusion over time that it might be a good idea to send Jesus as the centre of His purpose; it was *always* God's plan to do so. The idea of Jesus can be found throughout the Old Testament years before he was born – whether in the promises, in specific prophecies, or through symbolism and worked examples in the lives of faithful people who foreshadowed their Lord. The Old Testament is in its own way focused on the Lord Jesus Christ just as much as the New even though he hadn't yet been born when it was written. Having seen, then, this rhythm undergirding the entire Bible, it makes perfect sense to look at the Bible as one book rather than de-emphasising or dispensing with one part or other (whether the Old Testament or the New).

The life, death and resurrection of Jesus is so important that it is recorded four times in the four Gospel accounts. But really *the whole Bible* centres on Jesus' work. The Old Testament looked forward to him, predicted him, and presented the problems to which he stands as God's solution. The later books of the New Testament like the letters of Paul and the other New Testament writings elaborate on his life and his irreplaceable significance as the linchpin of God's great purpose to fill the earth with His glory. In the chapters to come it's only right, therefore, that we should focus on Jesus and his crucial role in God's purpose. When we have done that we can look at God's future plans to establish His kingdom right here upon earth.

Chapter 19

New leader

TO be in downtown New York City the night that President Obama was elected the first black president of the United States was a unique experience. In the midst of the financial crisis and deep scepticism about the Iraq war, there had come, seemingly from nowhere, a sense of optimism: the hope of change. Even those who disagreed with Obama's politics had to admit his eloquence as an orator and the attraction of the message; even those who were deeply sceptical were somehow swept along in the excitement of the moment – the sense of what might be. People were dancing in the streets, celebrating and enthusing one another about what they had just witnessed. The next morning, even small schoolchildren who never normally talked of politics were chatting excitedly on their way to school. The world was somehow caught up in the hope of change.

Concept and reality

Of course, the reality could never match that sense of hope and anticipation. Even Obama himself recognised it, warning how the road to economic recovery would be slow and hard. The purpose of referring to Obama's victory that night is not to comment on his politics or his subsequent performance, but to point out how the *concept* of new, fair, hopeful leadership was so attractive to people – even if we all know in practise that it is something no politician can ever fully deliver, no matter how hard they try.

We *want* change – we *ache* for it. We know the current political process is inadequate; we believe it *ought* to be possible to do it better, yet somehow we are always disappointed. We know, in our heart of hearts, that there must be right leadership somewhere, that the world *should* be fairer and more straightforward. But where can such leadership be found? Is there anywhere that the hope for change and the desire for new and strong leadership – captured so fleetingly at the excitement surrounding Obama's victory – can be delivered?

The answer is a very definite 'Yes'. Such leadership, the sort of leadership that fair-minded people crave, can indeed be found and will one day exist on the earth. It has been promised explicitly in the Bible. What we need is a new kind of leader, one who is like us in one sense, and yet so *un*like us in another, the one spoken of to Adam, to Abraham, to Moses and to David. We're talking, of course, about the Lord Jesus Christ, the promised future king of God's kingdom upon earth.

Credentials

But who was Jesus, what is so unique about him, and what makes him suitable for this special role when so many others, great though they may have been in their own individual ways, have failed?

First, Jesus is the world's most famous teacher and religious leader, and this alone would single him out even though there have certainly been other great teachers during the course of human history. Jesus is so much more than merely a teacher, however. He cannot simply be relegated to the role of a man who merely said some wise things. His birth, his life, his death, and his resurrection are all one-of-a-kind. His very *identity* as a human being is unique: he is not only a teacher but also the saviour of the world and the future king of God's kingdom. To talk merely of Jesus' unique teachings is also to stop short of mentioning one of his most distinctive attributes as a human – that, while fully exposed to all the temptations every human being faces, he committed no sin. This makes him utterly unique. There never has been, nor will there be, another like him.

In next two chapters we shall take a closer look at just three of these aspects: Jesus' unique identity, his ministry, and his role as God's ambassador. This will give us a good basis for turning in the following chapters to his death and resurrection.

Chapter 20

No ordinary man

THE Gospels make it plain that the birth of Jesus was absolutely unique. He was the son of Mary, but Jesus' conception came about miraculously by the power of God and not by the intervention of a man.[1] So Jesus was both human (as the son of Mary), and also the son of God. Interestingly the Bible draws a parallel between Adam, the first man who was also specifically created by God, and the Lord Jesus Christ, Adam's perfect counterpart. Just like Adam Jesus was a special creation of God, the one who would triumph where Adam failed. God often works with elaborate patterns in this way much as we can find intricate patterns and wonderful beauty in the natural world also.

Jesus' nature

Jesus' lineage through Mary is important because Mary is in the family line of King David of Old Testament fame, meaning that Jesus is one of David's descendants. This is important because key Bible prophecies had stated that one day a special son of David would sit on his throne in Jerusalem for ever. Jesus is the fulfilment of those Old Testament promises made to David, as well as the promises made to Adam and Eve, Abraham, Moses and Isaiah.

But to say that Jesus is the son of a woman is only half the story. Jesus was conceived by the Holy Spirit power of God, and therefore he is also the Son of God. This is incredibly important, and differentiates him from everyone else who has ever lived. Jesus is God's ambassador

---

1   Remember, we are talking about the Creator of the world here, so it is not really an obstacle for Him to cause a woman to become pregnant without intercourse or human intervention if He so chooses.

and perfect representative, and as His son is uniquely positioned to accurately reflect, portray and represent Him.

What does this dual-origin of Jesus (son of God and son of a woman) mean about his nature? Was he some sort of demi-god: half human and half god? The Bible is clear on this point. Jesus is a *man*. Take this verse, for instance:

> "For there is one God, and there is one mediator between God and men, *the man* Christ Jesus ..."   (1 Timothy 2:5)

Notice that Paul is very clear to distinguish between God and Jesus in this passage. There is one God, and He has a son, the man Christ Jesus. There are many passages that make a similar point.

Real temptations

The fact that Jesus is a man means that, during his earthly life he was subject to the same challenges and temptations which we face. He became tired, just as we do. He was afflicted by physical pain as we are. He aged as we age. He possessed the same temptable, corruptible, dying nature that we possess:

> "For we do not have a high priest who is unable to sympathise with our weaknesses, but one who in every respect has been tempted as we are, yet without sin."   (Hebrews 4:15)

This is very important for it makes his victory over sin and his refusal to give in to temptation all the more amazing and relevant to ourselves. One of the most unique things about Jesus is that, unlike us, he did no sin. If he were immune to pain and weakness then he wouldn't really be tempted in the same way that we are, and the fact that he did no sin would be of little interest to us because we could never relate to it. His victory over sin – the fact that he always said 'No!' to serving himself and going his own way – is so impressive and so noteworthy precisely because he fought the same fight that we do and yet refused to give in. He was always able to make the right choices, yet at the same time he has sympathy for us in our weaknesses because he knows how difficult it is to face them.

While Jesus was fully human (that is, he was not 'God' or 'a god'), he was also more like God than we are (as he himself said, 'I proceeded forth and came from God' (John 8:42, KJV) – none of us could say that in quite the same sense as Jesus!). A simple analogy of inheritance can perhaps help here. Humans generally inherit traits from both their parents, and if we think of that notion in the context of Jesus, it would make sense to assume he had some likeness to both his mother and his father.

Son of God

While it's tough to pinpoint *precisely* what that means (in the natural human desire to explain we must be careful of not saying more than the Bible does), there are some conclusions that we can draw. We have already drawn one from the Bible – that despite his dual origin, Jesus is fully human in terms of his essential nature. However, he likely also inherited traits from his father. We know that he spoke to his father regularly and directly, and it is likely that he had a more keenly developed moral and spiritual sense and a greater love for divine things as the Son of God than is often the case for us. We also know that God gave him powers to work miracles and to know what other people were thinking that we simply do not possess. There were therefore very unique attributes to Jesus even though they did not overwrite the reality of his fully human nature.

Although the Bible does not say so in quite so many words, this divine influence likely played an important role in enabling Jesus to carry out his mission, live a sinless life, and offer himself as a sacrifice for sin. Although we might think it *theoretically* possible that a regular human being could live a perfect life without sin, we know that practically speaking, this has never been done and never will be done. Jesus was human, but he was also the Son of God. He was able to win a battle in which we repeatedly fail – and we can say this without in any way minimising the reality of his struggle.

Chapter 21

Ministry and message

JESUS' ministry when he walked the earth was devoted to teaching people about God's ways and leading them to aspire to new heights of spiritual potential. But as he preached he was never too busy to care for the sick and attend to the practical needs of ordinary people. His ministry was characterised by the practical work of healing the sick on the one hand (a work which also carried a deeply significant spiritual meaning), and teaching about the future kingdom of God on the other.

Jesus' ministry

Jesus' teaching ministry was focused on God, on the coming kingdom, and on what sort of people we need to be in order to please God (we looked at one summary of his message back in chapter 10: our twofold duty to love God and put Him first, and to love our neighbour). His public ministry lasted three and a half years, and during it Jesus went about the land of Israel accompanied by his disciples so that he could teach people about repentance and the good news of the coming kingdom. It was a challenging and demanding message, but one which appealed to people because they could sense it was both idealistic and inspirational yet also thoroughly *right*. He spoke with authority and conviction which was quite different to the woolly philosophising and empty ritual of his peers; he commanded people's respect and admiration. He spoke a simple message, but one which had tremendous depth. He spoke of ideals, and of how God would have us behave. He spoke of the need to repent and change our ways so as to get back into a good relationship with God.

But Jesus didn't just *talk*. He also *did* amazing things: working miracles, healing the sick, feeding the hungry, and giving signs to demonstrate that he was who he claimed to be – the Son of God sent into the world to save sinners. His works of healing and his concern for the poor, the outcast and the down-trodden and his overturning of social norms and conventions showed that he meant what he said – that loving God with all one's heart and loving one's neighbour really is what it is all about.

The man is the message

Some people admit that Jesus was a great teacher but want to stop at that rather than go any further. If we really engage with the words of Jesus, however, we will find that he will not allow us this option.

The point is that Jesus did not merely teach a message – he *was* the message, the very embodiment of it. We have all met people who say one thing and do another; Jesus was the very opposite of this. He lived what he preached and showed by practical example what it means to truly love God and to truly love one's fellow human beings. He showed by giving his very life what true dedication and sacrifice to God really means.

Jesus was God's living, breathing representative on the earth – nothing less. An ambassador of a foreign country can speak for his country and its leaders up to a point, but there will be some matters which are above his pay-grade, so to speak, and which he will have to refer back to the prime minister, president or monarch whom he represents. By contrast, Jesus was God's *perfect* representative, the ultimate ambassador. He knew instinctively and intrinsically what God's view on a subject would be and what He would want. He always did his Father's will, and he always saw things as God saw them. As Jesus said:

"Whoever has seen me has seen the Father."   (John 14:9)

This means that if you saw and experienced Jesus – if you really came to know him – then you could understand more than any mere teaching would allow what God was like. This was the sense in which Jesus was God's word (His purpose, plan and power) made flesh (John 1:14). The great news is that we can still get to know him today – that's why there are four different Gospel accounts of his life recorded in the Bible, each one giving a different perspective on his great work, and why so much of both the New Testament and the Old is all about him.

Jesus was the one who God sent into the world to save men and women from their sinfulness and its deathly consequences. His very name embodies this, for the name 'Jesus' means 'God saves'. Jesus spoke of himself as the way (to God), the door (back into fellowship in God's house), the truth (about God) and the life (without Jesus, there is only death to look forward to). This is why Jesus is so critical to God's purpose, and this is why Jesus could say:

"No one comes to the Father except through me."   (John 14:6)

There is no way around it, then, coming to understand Jesus' identity, his mission and his message is absolutely crucial to understanding God's great purpose. Having explored a little of these topics therefore we can now move to the incident in Jesus' life which marks the very centre of world history, the defining moment of God's plan and of Jesus' work: the crucifixion and resurrection.

Chapter 22

The crucifixion

IT might seem all very well to admire Jesus and even to applaud his perfect life, recognising his unique identity as God's ambassador and son. But what about his suffering, crucifixion and death? What did those things do to help, and were they really necessary? What did Jesus' crucifixion and death really achieve, and what difference does it make whether or not he was raised from the dead? These questions are pivotal, and we shall take our time considering them in the next few chapters.

It can be very helpful to think about the death of Jesus as both a human and a divine drama, an event which undoubtedly took place as a historical fact, but one which is more than merely 'something that once happened a long time ago', a curiosity of history. The crucifixion was in the biggest of senses a *statement* – a statement and demonstration of epic, world-changing proportions – a statement communicating a profound message about all the characters involved: about human nature, about God, about the nature of true love and sacrifice, and about God's great plan for the world.

What men did

First consider the human players: those who brought Jesus to be killed (the Jews) and those who crucified him (the Romans). Why was it, in human terms, that people wanted him to meet such a fate – who would have done this to him? What was it that so offended and angered people to take them to this extreme?

Ironically it was Jesus' own people the Jews who brought him to the Roman governor Pontius Pilate to ask for him to be crucified. His own people – including some of those who had once adored him as their hero – ultimately rejected him and bayed for his blood. In doing so they rejected the very one who was sent to be their Saviour, the long-promised Messiah. Incited by their leaders' jealousy and their desire to protect their own power-base, they clamoured for his torture and death.

There is something deeply disturbing about this – that God should send His very own son to be His people's saviour and that they should reject and even kill the one He sent in this most despicable fashion. It says something truly frightening about the propensity for evil that lies within the hearts of human beings. Yet this abominable demonstration of humans at their worst is at the same time fully in keeping with what we saw about human nature back in chapters 12 through to 14 (especially chapter 13). The Jewish leaders felt insecure, jealous and threatened, and they allowed these feelings to grow to such an extent that they would stop at nothing to remove him. By doing so they demonstrated the dark side of human behaviour at its worst.

But Jesus was also put to death by the Romans who carried out the Jews' wishes; the Bible lays blame at their door as well. Pontius Pilate himself was motivated by fear and by the desire to protect his own position of power even though he knew Jesus to be innocent. For their part, the Roman soldiers who scourged, flogged and crucified him were doing no more than a day's work – but what an unspeakably cruel work it was as they suspended their fellow-feeling and compassion for the life of another, perhaps even taking perverse satisfaction in the power they wielded as they humiliated him. This too tells us much about our nature – the crass insensitivity and cruelty we can be capable of, the gang spirit and the way in which we can even take enjoyment in others' pain.

What this means is that the whole world – Jews and non-Jews alike – is effectively implicated in these awful events. If the Jewish leaders represent religious power then the Roman leaders represent political power, while the crowds represent ordinary people. They were *all* involved in Jesus' death and human nature as a whole is implicated and condemned.

Sin exposed

Think about it this way. The cruelty of betraying, flogging and crucifying this innocent man is itself a perfect demonstration of what sin is, and what humans can be like. *This* is the cruelty that humans are capable of. And here, as Jesus hangs on the cross, the evil of sin and human behaviour is writ large.

Many writers and thinkers over the centuries have recognised this point – that Jesus' death effectively implicates them and indeed all humanity. As a example here are some of the words of bluesman B. B. King and U2 in their song 'When love comes to town':

"I was there when they crucified my Lord
I held the scabbard when the soldier drew his sword.
I threw the dice when they pierced his side
– But I've seen love conquer the great divide."

Or again, from a popular hymn:

"Behold the man upon a cross,
My sin upon his shoulders;
Ashamed, I hear my mocking voice
Call out among the scoffers.
It was my sin that held him there
Until it was accomplished;
His dying breath has brought me life –
I know that it is finished."

The death of Jesus *exposes* sin and it exposes human nature; it shows it for what it is in all its awfulness, and shows why something awe-*ful* – something awe-*inspiring* – needs to be done about it. Human nature is condemned and its need for redemption demonstrated by the very events we see unfolding at Jesus' death – *but the solution is also revealed at the same time.* In the face of human cruelty the love of Jesus is transcendent as Jesus is lifted high on the cross, literally and symbolically above those who killed him. The love of Jesus is not defeated; in fact it conquers because everyone knows in their heart of hearts that it is the better way, stronger and more powerful than those low weapons of cruelty humans exercised towards him. Its power as the right and living way, the way which will give rise to life, is sealed definitively by God when, very shortly, He raises His son from the dead. For a few short days human sinfulness seemed to have triumphed as Jesus lay in the tomb. But while it did indeed give rise to death, the love of God and the love of Jesus give birth to a new and transcendent life on the morning of resurrection. Hatred brings death, but love brings life out of even the blackest night.

Approaching the cross

And what of ourselves? When we each in our mind's eye approach the cross of Christ there is much to reflect upon. We see the dark side of our own nature in the actions of those who killed him and we find ourselves implicated for the cruelty, selfishness and jealousy that we have sometimes shown. We see our need for salvation – that we need saving even from our very selves, our own humanity – and we see the need for a new start, a better way. When we look at Jesus we see just what that way must be. It lies in giving instead of taking, in thinking of others rather than ourselves and being prepared to sacrifice ourselves for them. It consists in trusting in God and resisting our inclinations to fight, whether it be through self-preservation or blame.

We find here in the Lord Jesus one who can take our burdens and our guilt and bear them away, putting them to death on his cross. We are each carrying on our shoulders the burden of sin and its inevitable consequence in death – carrying around that weight of guilt and sin and the toll it takes on our lives both physically and emotionally. Jesus takes our burden upon himself, bearing our sins on our behalf, and puts them to death on the cross.

Chapter 23

The greatest gift

IF Jesus' enemies show us what human nature is like at its worst and why sin needs to be condemned, what do Jesus' own actions and motives show? And what of the God and Father beholding all this – what is His part and His response to these shocking events?

The gift of Jesus

The death of Jesus turns human values on their head and demonstrates divine standards. Jesus' actions show him *surrendering* his life and *giving* it as a sacrifice for others. Let's think about both of these ideas – the concepts of surrendering and sacrificial giving. It's human nature to defend ourselves, whether physically ('fight or flight') or emotionally (by making excuses or blaming someone else). It's basic to our nature to self-protect and deflect blame even when we are completely in the wrong. The beauty and the wonder of what Jesus did is that it was the exact opposite of this even though he had done nothing wrong! If there was anyone who could have fought or fled, it was him – he had the power of God at his disposal. But Jesus didn't. He turned a history of escalation and vengeance-seeking on its head by making a conscious decision to *give* his life for us rather than *take* matters into his own hands. As Jesus himself said:

> "Greater love has no one than this, that someone lay down his life for his friends." (John 15:13)

There is nothing more precious that one can give than life itself. And there is nothing more precious than the life of Jesus. How so? Because his was a *sinless* life. It thus had much more value than our own lives, since in our case death is no more than we deserve because of the sins we have committed.

But the death of Jesus is not only a gift, it is also a sacrifice – a precious life willingly surrendered in order to secure a better life both for himself and for us. It is no ordinary sacrifice, however; it is the ultimate sacrifice made with his very life-blood, a sacrifice in which Jesus as our representative pays the price for human sin. Jesus' shed blood makes possible a new covenant between God and man based on faith (from us), on love and righteousness (from Christ), and on mercy and forgiveness (from God). [1]

Because death is the price or consequence of sin and the purpose of Jesus' sacrifice is to bear away and destroy our sins we can perhaps start to understand another dimension of his sacrifice. He bears our sins and crucifies them so that they are gone for good. Not only so, the corruptible, temptable nature that we bear (and which he also shared) is crucified as well. This was a sacrifice that only he could make; we ourselves couldn't offer it because our death would be no more than we deserved as a result of our sins; what was unique about Jesus' sacrifice was that he offered it after having lived a perfect life in God's sight. *Everyone* who believes can therefore benefit from Jesus' death; it is the doorway to a transformation of human beings' potential in God's sight. Because of Jesus' sinless life and perfect sacrifice God was abundantly eager to raise him again from death to a new kind of life. By giving up the most precious thing he could for the benefit of others Jesus unlocks the possibility of a new paradigm of existence in God's sight.

What God did

What, then, about the death of Jesus from God's perspective?

The bottom line is this: if Jesus gave the most precious thing that *he* could for our salvation (his own life), then so did God: He gave His only begotten son. God couldn't give His own life since He is by definition immortal and can neither die nor surrender His being given

---

1   God's actions also manifest both love and righteousness of course, just like those of Jesus.

that He is the ground and centre of all things. But He gave the most precious thing that He could as an illustration of His willingness to save – His only son. Indeed, many of us who are parents would say that we would rather see ourselves suffer than witness the suffering of our children – meaning that God's gift of His own son is the most precious He could possibly have made as a token of His love. This, then, is the measure of His desire to forgive and take us back. This is the measure of His love, a point made in perhaps the most famous passage of the entire Bible:

"For God so loved the world, that he gave his only son, that whoever believes in him should not perish but have eternal life."

(John 3:16)

It's important to reflect on the full import of these words. God *gave* Jesus and initiated the possibility of forgiveness because He loved us. It is not the case that, after the fall of mankind, God is simply mad at us and has to be appeased by Jesus' death. Instead (and by total contrast with that idea) it is God who initiates the possibility of salvation, carefully planning for the birth and sacrifice of His son. He does so because He loves us, not because He hates us. What He hates is sin, and the death of Jesus is God's powerful way of expressing both the awfulness of sin and also His love of mankind and desire to save them. He allows His son – no *gives* him – to pay the price of human sinfulness and the curse of human nature.

The righteousness of God

The death of Jesus also declares the righteousness of God. It does this both by condemning sin (showing how bad it is, the consequences to which it leads, and that God is right to say that it is wrong), and by showing the right way to behave (Jesus' perfect life and love held high as a perfect example). Jesus illustrates the goodness and righteousness of God – that what God had said was right and that human beings ought to have gone His way. Once this has been recognised God can begin to forge a relationship with us on a new and better basis.

Because he had no sins of his own to die for Jesus is able to take our sins upon himself and bear them to the cross where they are condemned and put to death. But Jesus also condemns human nature – that corruptible and dying nature which he shared with us – by surrendering it and giving it up on the cross, putting it to death where it belongs. Instead of trusting in himself as we so often do, Jesus instead gives back his life to God, trusting in Him to grant him a new life on the glorious day of resurrection which is soon to follow.

Ultimately sin and death stand in the way between God and man. God cannot fill the earth with His glory while there is sin and corruption, and the world cannot be populated with immortal sinners. So there has to be death. But the death of Jesus – unique, because of the sinless life he led – opens the door to new terms of business: a new paradigm, a new relationship between God and man and the future hope of a life untarnished by weakness and pain. It is not death as an end in itself that we see when we consider the crucifixion; it is death as a gateway to a new kind of life – life on new terms with God as our Heavenly Father.

Chapter 24

Resurrection

THE principle can be seen in the dying of each day into night and in the dawning of the new as the sun rises. It can be seen in the changing of the seasons as year by year winter descends like a death, and then spring awakens the earth once more to a glorious new beginning. It can be seen in the hibernation of animals and their re-emergence, in the falling of the leaves and the budding of the new when spring comes round once more. It is the principle of rebirth – the principle of resurrection.

Only the beginning ...

When we think of all these precedents in nature it is obvious that Jesus' death could never have been the end. Far from it. If all we had was a dead saviour to remember where would be the hope and where the salvation? There wouldn't be any; there would just be ... death. On the contrary, Jesus' death is a deliberate doorway to a new life. He surrendered his old life – the temptable, corruptible, dying one which he knew could never be the ultimate route to a life in full fellowship with God – in order to receive a new and better one.

Nature itself points the way and illustrates the pattern. When an animal retreats into its lair for hibernation, when autumn fades into winter or when a caterpillar forms itself into a chrysalis, this is not the end-game. It is instead the doorway to something new and better. God has built the very principles of death and resurrection into nature as if to show us His way of working – it is the same principle in both the natural world and in the spiritual sphere. God's plan to save men and women and to restore the world and fill it with His glory all works through the principle of death and resurrection. The spiritual pattern by which He will save men and women is enshrined in the very structure of the natural world He has created.

The Bible says that after his death, the grave *could not hold* Jesus – that's how it is when sin's hold over us has been destroyed, and it is a mark of how eager God was to save His son for the perfect life that He had lived and the wonderful sacrifice that He had made. In return for surrendering and giving his mortal life God raised Jesus to a new and better life: a life no longer subject to temptation, aging and death.

Resurrection

True hope for the future therefore does not lie in Jesus' death *per se*, but in the resurrection which followed it. If Jesus had remained in the grave then there would be no hope. The point is that because he sacrificed his life and gave himself to God on our behalf, God raised him from the dead and gave him a new and better life.

While this idea of Jesus' resurrection from death might initially seem a little too far removed from our experience of reality to take seriously, we ought first to try a little thought experiment. Imagine for a second that we had never seen or heard of a caterpillar wrapping itself into a cocoon and then transforming itself into a butterfly. If we had never heard of it before and someone showed us a caterpillar and a butterfly, telling us that, in a relatively short period of time, one would quite literally transform into the other, we would consider them mad – completely out of their mind. We wouldn't even *begin* to believe them because the possibility of such a thing would be completely outside our experience and would seem utterly and crazily impossible. And yet – bringing back now the knowledge that we do in fact have – we know that this bizarre and remarkable thing does indeed happen, and happens all the time: a caterpillar really can turn into a butterfly. Now if such a thing can happen – despite the apparent unlikeliness of it – why should we be surprised that God, who has created the entire world and has made us in His image, should raise His son from the dead should He choose to do so? Put like that it doesn't really seem so remarkable at all. It actually starts to feel *necessary* and *inevitable*. Why would God *not* do so, especially in the light of the sinless life, perfect obedience, and absolute self-sacrifice that His son had just shown?

Resurrection is therefore not an optional extra to a Christian faith – something reserved only for those with a greater-than-average helping of credulity. No, it is intrinsic to the Bible's message and to the purpose of God. If God can bring nature into existence in the first place then He can certainly raise the dead if He chooses. Aside from resurrection there isn't any hope held out to men and women in the Bible – this *is* the hope for the future, and without it there is nothing, as the Apostle Paul himself states:

"And if Christ has not been raised, your faith is futile and you are still in your sins." (1 Corinthians 15:17)

Evidence

So why would we believe in Jesus' resurrection and choose to re-shape our lives around it aside from the many examples of symbolic death and rebirth we find in nature? Is it an arbitrary view to which there is no logic and only faith? Not a bit of it. The case for believing that the tomb was indeed empty because Jesus had been raised to new life is surprisingly compelling.

Christianity is not a religion which limped cautiously onto the world stage and gradually picked up momentum over time. No, it entered human history in explosive fashion and did so as a *historical* religion, a religion based on events that were believed by its first proponents to have literally taken place and which were backed up by extensive eyewitness accounts. Chief among those events was the physical, bodily resurrection of the Lord Jesus Christ. What started as a tiny group of demoralised disciples in the immediate aftermath of Jesus' death suddenly erupted into a religion in which the good news travelled like wildfire through the Roman empire. Countless men and women suffered persecution and accepted martyrdom for the things that they believed and had seen. How could this have happened? This dramatic about-turn and rocket-fire launch of the Gospel message into the world on the basis of eyewitness testimony could only have come about because there actually *was* an empty tomb and because there *were* hundreds of eyewitnesses who saw Jesus after his resurrection before he ascended to heaven. Many people gave up their lives for their faith not because of hearsay or because of some abstract philosophy but because they themselves had personally seen him after his death. They were therefore able to give powerful, convicted testimony to others to whom they preached. While there are certainly other theories (perhaps Jesus just swooned on the cross, or perhaps the disciples stole the body and claimed he had been raised – these are two of the most common), none of them adequately account for the historical facts. The literal resurrection of Christ is the explanation that best fits the facts of the spread of early Christianity and the historical sources we have. [1]

Resurrection in the future

But what is the relevance of Jesus' resurrection for ourselves? This is indeed a crucial question, and the great news is that resurrection is not something that was only for the Lord Jesus Christ. While he was certainly the first to experience a bodily resurrection of the type that he did, the wonderful truth is that God offers exactly the same hope of resurrection when Christ returns to the earth to those who die with faith in him. Jesus' resurrection sets the pattern for all those who believe in God: it's as if right now we are living the life of caterpillars, waiting for that wonderful butterfly stage when by God's grace we are raised from the dead at Jesus' return.

If we approach God in the right way, though we may die, God will one day raise us from the dead and give us a new life – new in both quality and quantity – when Jesus comes again to establish God's kingdom. When we die we are really dead – that's the end of us (for

1   See Appendix 2 (page 137) for further reading suggestions.

the time being at least); we do not float away and exist in some other realm or as a disembodied spirit. The consistent message of the Bible is that what lies beyond for the believer is not an ethereal existence who-knows-where, but rather the hope of bodily resurrection to live in God's presence on the earth which He has prepared as our home.

When we die – if we die in faith and in hope – it is more like a sleep as we quietly wait in the grave for the wonderful resurrection morning that God has promised. Time now, then, to turn our attention from the past of Jesus' first coming, death and resurrection, and towards the bright hope for the future when he comes back to the earth again. We have covered the first half of the Gospel message – the things concerning the Lord Jesus Christ; now it is time to turn to what is yet to come: the second half – the things concerning the kingdom of God.

Chapter 25

Kingdom come

WHEN the angel Gabriel told Mary that her son Jesus would one day be a king, he wasn't saying anything about the promised Messiah which was new. The idea that God planned a unique future king for the earth was not something dreamed up by Gabriel or the New Testament writers; the idea is rooted firmly in the Old Testament, the first and largest part of the Bible. Nor was Gabriel saying something which would be true in only an abstract or spiritual sense. He was announcing something which will literally come about on the earth in the future. Let's take a closer look in this, the first of four chapters which focus on the future kingdom which God plans to set up.

Gabriel's prophecy

First we should look specifically at what the angel Gabriel had to say before Jesus was born:

> "And the angel said to [Mary], 'Do not be afraid, Mary, for you have found favour with God. And behold, you will conceive In your womb and bear a son, and you shall call his name Jesus. He will be great and will be called the Son of the Most High. And the Lord God will give to him the throne of his father David, and he will reign over the house of Jacob for ever, and of his kingdom there will be no end.' ... And the angel answered her, 'The Holy Spirit will come upon you, and the power of the Most High will overshadow you; therefore the child to be born will be called holy – the Son of God.'"
> (Luke 1:30-33,35)

King David would probably be considered the greatest and the archetypal Israelite king. He had a literal throne in Jerusalem from which he reigned, and many of the surrounding nations were subject to him – although perhaps his most defining feature was that he was described as 'a man after God's own heart' which was what made him such a great king. Notice that Gabriel deliberately connects Jesus' future reign with David's. Just as David had a literal throne on which he sat, so too Jesus will have a throne – he will inherit the throne of David, no less. He will be David's descendent (as Jesus indeed was, through his mother Mary).

So Jesus will be king over a literal kingdom on earth and will reign from Jerusalem on David's throne. That's why it makes sense, for instance, that in the famous 'Lord's Prayer' Jesus should have taught us to pray,

> "Thy kingdom come. Thy will be done *in earth*, as it is in heaven."
> (Matthew 6:10, KJV)

God's kingdom will be on earth and Jesus will be its king, just as David once was king. At that time God's will and ways will be put into action upon the earth in a way which will make His kingdom completely different to the governments, cultures and kingdoms present in the world today. In that day God's will indeed will be done on earth, as it is in heaven. It will be a kingdom of peace and goodness, a time when there will be justice and fairness for all with no exploitation of people or mis-distribution of the earth's resources.

Great though David was, he was not perfect. Jesus will far surpass him, for he will reign for ever (Gabriel says so, very clearly, and there are plenty of other passages which say the same). How is this possible? Because he is the Son of God. Because God raised him from the dead to die no more and gave him a new kind of life beyond anything that the rest of us have yet experienced. And because God's plan is to send him back to the earth again to be its king.

An everlasting kingdom

God made the point about the eternity of His future kingdom through the prophet Daniel writing about 2,500 years ago:

"And in the days of those kings the God of heaven will set up a kingdom that shall never be destroyed, nor shall the kingdom be left to another people. It shall break in pieces all these kingdoms and bring them to an end, and it shall stand for ever ..."

(Daniel 2:44)

The kingdom that God is planning will be universal and all-encompassing. It will be a kingdom which will not only differ in *quantity* (it will be everlasting and worldwide), but also in *quality*. It will have a perfect king who will judge all things correctly, one who will ensure that God's ways and wishes are put into action throughout the world.

Chapter 26

On earth as it is in heaven

THE earth on which we live now is certainly an incredible place – a place of beauty and grandeur, a place perfectly suited to human existence:

> "... The LORD who created the heavens (he is God!), who formed the earth and made it (he established it; he did not create it empty [i.e., in vain], he formed it to be inhabited!) ..." (Isaiah 45:18)

It makes sense, then, that God's purpose for the future does not centre around a 'happy hunting ground' somewhere else, an ethereal existence in heaven, or a spiritual 'out-of-body' life of some kind. Instead God's purpose centres on the earth He has created as the habitat for mankind. His future plan is to set up His kingdom right here so that He can have the relationship with men and women that He has sought from the beginning.

The right location

Lest there be any doubt about this point (and since it's quite an important one), it's worth us quickly looking at some further evidence which establishes that God's future kingdom will be here on the earth:

> "Blessed are the meek, for they shall **inherit the earth**."
>
> (Matthew 5:5)

> "For the evildoers shall be cut off, but those who wait for the LORD shall **inherit the land**. In just a little while, the wicked will be no more; though you look carefully at his place, he will not be there. But the meek shall **inherit the land** and delight themselves in abundant peace ... for those blessed by the LORD shall **inherit**

the land, but those cursed by him shall be cut off."

(Psalm 37:9-11,22)[1]

There's not much value in 'inheriting the earth' if the bright future God has planned for His creatures is to take place somewhere else!

Or again, even more clearly:

"And the LORD will be **king over all the earth**. On that day the Lord will be one and his name one." (Zechariah 14:9)

This fits in perfectly with what we have seen from the promises to David – that Jesus will reign from Jerusalem for ever. Here is another prophecy that picks up on this:

"At that time Jerusalem shall be called the throne of the LORD, and all nations shall gather to it, to the presence of the LORD in Jerusalem, and they shall no more stubbornly follow their own evil heart." (Jeremiah 3:17)

It's fascinating that even today Jerusalem should be the centre of so much political and religious conflict. No other city can lay claim to such contention, since Jerusalem is considered a holy site by no less than three of the world's major religious traditions (Christianity, Judaism, and Islam). There it is – right there at the very centre of the map of the world – and there it stands embattled in confrontation which is both military, political and religious. Yet the Old Testament prophets, while foreseeing further suffering, political tension and war in the Middle East before Jesus' kingdom is finally set up, ultimately speak of a time when Jews, Christians, and Arabs will all unite to worship God at Jerusalem. The Jew-Arab conflict will one day be resolved, the Bible is saying. Both Arabs, Jews and Christians, irrevocably estranged though they may now seem to be, will be united with one voice to worship God at Jerusalem. It is a remarkable image recorded more

---

1   This passage also explains that wicked people and people who do not want to follow God's ways will have no place in the kingdom which is to come. They will have had their time and opportunity, and when their lives are over they will simply die; they will have had their mortal lives as a gift from God and that will be the end of them.

than two thousand years ago, yet one which remains staggeringly graphic, relevant and hopeful in today's fractured world.

Ideal king

In sum, the Bible teaches that Jesus will be king over God's worldwide kingdom and will reign from Jerusalem for ever. So say both the Old and New Testaments with clear and unified voice. He will be a king like no other the world has ever known, more wise and more capable than any leader who has preceded him. There will be no more miscarriage of justice, no more unfairness, corruption and abuse of power. God will empower His son to transform our world into the world that God had originally planned it to be. As the prophet Isaiah put it:

> "Behold, a king will reign in righteousness ... like a hiding place from the wind, a shelter from the storm, like streams of water in a dry place, like the shade of a great rock in a weary land ..."
>
> (Isaiah 32:1,2)

Chapter 27

The return of the king

IN order to be king, Jesus must first return to the earth. This will take place at a time of considerable international turmoil, war, and political unrest. The Bible teaches that many nations will be gathered in a military attack against Israel, and as Jesus returns, the Jews will at last recognise him as the Messiah they denied for so long.

Nations in upheaval

In his Olivet prophecy, a famous passage in which Jesus lays out some of the events that will take place prior to his return, he describes a time of trouble such as never was, "men's hearts failing them for fear …" (Luke 21:26).

For the follower of Jesus, however, there is no need to fear. A Bible-believer knows that this time of tribulation is coming, and will recognise it not as a cause for panic but rather as a sign that Jesus' return is near. God is in control of world affairs, and He is delicately balancing the relationships between the nations to lead to the time when it will be right for Jesus to come back.

In one place these tensions in international affairs are described as 'birth pains'. Every woman knows that without medical intervention, childbirth can be extremely painful. However, that painful process gives rise to one of the greatest wonders that human experience can offer: the joy of a new child. It is very helpful to think of the coming geopolitical upheaval in just that way. It will be like the labour pains which precede the arrival of the wonderful new beginning of God's kingdom.

Of course some nations and some exponents of certain political and religious ideologies will not necessarily bow willingly to the authority of Jesus when he returns. The initial phase of the establishment of God's kingdom will therefore involve the subduing of those powers. God has given mankind hundreds and thousands of years to be ostensibly in control of his own destiny – allowing humans the free will to establish kingdoms and bureaucracies, coups and routs. By the time of Jesus' return, man will have had his chance at doing this his own way. Now it will be God's turn to show how it should be done, by means of His son Jesus as His king and perfect representative.

Promises of Jesus' return

When he was raised from death after his crucifixion, Jesus ascended to be with his Father until the time would be ripe for the establishment of God's kingdom. In the meantime God is allowing the good news of hope to spread in the earth, giving men and women the opportunity to turn to Him while in the meantime society as a whole continues to plough its own furrow.

When Jesus ascended to heaven, there was a clear message that he would come back again:

> "And while [the disciples] were gazing into heaven as [Jesus ascended], behold, two men stood by them in white robes, and said, 'Men of Galilee, why do you stand looking into heaven? This Jesus, who was taken up from you into heaven, will come in the same way as you saw him go into heaven.'" (Acts 1:10,11)

And there are plenty of other passages which talk about his return, for instance:

> "For as the lightning comes from the east and shines as far as the west, so will be the coming of the Son of Man." (Matthew 24:27)

Jesus therefore told us to live our lives now preparing for his coming, watching and waiting for his return:

> "Therefore, stay awake, for you do not know on what day your Lord is coming." (Matthew 24:42; see also Mark 13:33)

A new life

When Jesus comes back to the earth there will be a resurrection of the dead (we touched on this briefly when we thought about Jesus' own resurrection) and also a judgement for those who know enough about God's ways to be in a position to choose whether to live responsibly before Him or not. While we only have space to mention these topics in passing, we should observe briefly that there are no 'immortal souls' in the Bible, no sense that when we die we somehow exist outside our bodies in another realm. When we die, we are dead – that's it! But – and it's a critical 'but' – there is nevertheless a hope. It is the hope of resurrection in which the dead are raised – in their bodies, on the earth, as human beings.

For those who have believed in God and sought to please Him by the way they have lived their lives, there will, by God's grace, be a wonderful change that takes place in their bodies and to the nature of their existence as they enter God's kingdom. The Apostle Paul describes this in his letter to believers who lived in Corinth. He is writing about the resurrection of those who God accepts in the judgement:

"Behold! I tell you a mystery. We shall not all sleep, but we shall all be changed, in a moment, in the twinkling of an eye, at the last trumpet. For the trumpet will sound, and the dead will be raised imperishable, and we shall be changed. For this perishable body must put on the imperishable, and this mortal body must put on immortality. When the perishable puts on the imperishable, and the mortal puts on immortality, then shall come to pass the saying that is written: 'Death is swallowed up in victory.' 'O death, where is your victory? O death, where is your sting?'"

(1 Corinthians 15:51-55)

This, then, is the answer to one of life's biggest questions: is there an afterlife, and what happens to us when we die? In the *Financial Times* magazine every weekend there is an interview with a famous person in which they are asked whether or not they believe in an afterlife. A large number say that they do, reflecting a common belief in wider society. But there is usually a lack of certainty about it and a distinct lack of colour and clarity about what form any sort of existence beyond our current lives might take. Fortunately the Bible leaves us in no doubt because it clearly holds out to us the possibility of an immortal life here on earth in which we will share in perfect fellowship with our maker and with one another in God's kingdom.

This will be a life with no more cancer, no more Alzheimer's, no more estrangement between human beings and their God, and no more infighting amongst themselves. There will be no more suffering or pain for those who are raised from death and found pleasing to God. Indeed, it's not just about *not* having this or that; we will also be empowered to use our capacities – whether physical, intellectual, emotional or spiritual – in ways far beyond what we are currently capable of. Perhaps we can liken it to an unlocking of all our full potential as human beings – perhaps abilities and levels of experience we were theoretically capable of but never able or responsible enough to properly utilise. It's an incredible prospect during which the prime directive will finally be fulfilled: God's glory and the knowledge of it will finally fill the whole earth and the human beings who live there will finally be seen in all their full potential.

Chapter 28

The to-do list

ONCE Jesus' rule is established in the earth there will be a huge amount of work to do. After millennia of man's rule and mismanagement, the earth will need to be restored to its former and better state: cleaning up pollution, resolving institutional evil and oppression, and getting the world working In a way which is in accordance with God's commands. Human society will have to be restructured in fundamentally new ways to be centred upon God and His agenda. Everyone will be impacted by this.

There will be an enormous task of education necessary for the world's population so that they can understand what God wants from human beings and how they should live before Him. It will be an incredibly exciting time as the earth's resources are re-apportioned and correctly utilised.

Life transformed

There are many amazing passages in the Bible which describe in poetic terms just how wonderful God's kingdom will be. We'll take a look at three of them, all drawn from the prophet Isaiah. Right at the beginning of his long prophecy, Isaiah lays out a statement of intent from God:

> "It shall come to pass in the latter days that the mountain of the house of the LORD shall be established as the highest of the mountains, and shall be lifted up above the hills; and all the nations shall flow to it, and many peoples shall come, and say, 'Come, let us go up to the mountain of the LORD, to the house of the God of Jacob, that he may teach us his ways and that we may walk in his paths.' For out of Zion shall go the law, and the word of the LORD from Jerusalem." (Isaiah 2:2-4)

This passage is saying that in God's kingdom the world will be centred upon *God* (whereas most previous human kingdoms have been centred upon man or some kind of human ideology, even if they have claimed otherwise). People will have a centre for their lives, a purpose, and they will want to learn about God and His ways so that they can align their lives with Him and experience the joy of connection with the infinite that they have never before experienced. They will finally be able to be in tune with Him, and will find this an immense source of fulfilment and joy. People will no longer have to debate right and wrong; they will no longer talk about 'what's right for you' versus 'what's right for me'. There will be no more 'relative truth'. God's word and law will go forth from Jesus' throne in Jerusalem.

New standards

Here's another passage which describes some of the benefits of the kingdom:

> "Then the eyes of the blind shall be opened, and the ears of the deaf unstopped; then shall the lame man leap like a deer, and the tongue of the mute sing for joy. For waters break forth in the wilderness, and streams in the desert ... And a highway shall be there, and it shall be called the Way of Holiness; the unclean shall not pass over it. It shall belong to those who walk on the way; even if they are fools, they shall not go astray ... And the ransomed of the LORD shall return and come to Zion with singing; everlasting joy shall be upon their heads; they shall obtain gladness and joy, and sorrow and sighing shall flee away." (Isaiah 35:5,6,8,10)

It will be a time when the effects of aging and sickness will be drastically reduced, a time of overflowing joy and awakening.

Known unknowns

All this being said, there are still many things we do not know about the kingdom and many of the questions we may want to ask about the details would result predominantly in speculation. To what extent will there be use of automation and technology, for instance? Will people drive cars? What will they eat, and will some things be outlawed? What new spiritual powers or technologies will God enable us to use, and what hitherto unused capacities of our brains will be unlocked? It's widely thought that humans only use about 10-20% of their overall brainpower right now and it's very exciting to think what we might be capable of were our full capacities to be unlocked – just the sort of thing that God might have in store for human beings in the kingdom age. We just don't know the answers to these questions, and we are so limited by our current perception and experience of the world that it is hard for us to think in an informed way outside of that box.

What we do know, however, is that God always does that which is right, and He knows how to give His creatures what is best for them. Whatever He has in store for us in His kingdom we know will be thoroughly good because it comes from Him and He has proved that He can be trusted.

And with that, our final passage from Isaiah:

"For behold, I create new heavens and a new earth [i.e., a new start on the earth, a new world order], and the former things shall not be remembered or come into mind. But be glad and rejoice forever in that which I create; for behold, I create Jerusalem to be a joy, and her people to be a gladness. I will rejoice in Jerusalem and be glad in my people; no more shall be heard in it the sound of weeping and the cry of distress." (Isaiah 65:17-19)

Beyond this exciting phase there are two fascinating passages which give a tantalising glimpse of what God has in store. First, the Apostle Paul says that ultimately God will be 'all in all'. This seems to imply a closer fellowship, relationship or integration between God and His creatures than currently exists. Similarly, the Apostle Peter speaks of a time when humans will be 'partakers of the divine nature'. Back in Eden, Adam and Eve thought that by taking the forbidden fruit they would become 'like God'. But it didn't turn out that way; breaking God's commands is not the way to become like Him! Ultimately, however, there is nothing God wants more than to be revealed in and among the people He has created. His plan is to make Himself manifest in them, even allowing them, at the end of time, to share His very nature. This will be the ultimate reality.

Chapter 29

Belief

HAVING explored the Bible's answers to our most important needs both as individuals and as a society it's now time to turn to another very important issue: if this message that we have been considering is true, what should we do about it? How do we receive this salvation God is promising and how can we be sure that, when Jesus returns, we will be welcomed into God's kingdom? Is there something we need to do to earn it? Or do we just sit back and relax, and trust that everything will be okay?

The remaining chapters of this book are therefore all about *response*. In this chapter we'll consider how salvation is a gift from God which cannot be earned. But that doesn't mean that there is nothing for us to do! The first thing we need to do is *believe* what God has said, but beyond that there are other crucial steps of transformation which God also wants us to take, along with a whole new way of life He wants us to lead. Far from being a burden, this new way of life turns out to be not only liberating but also purposeful and inspiring.

Earning and receiving

The only thing we deserve or *earn* as sinful human beings who have fallen short of God's standard is death. Not very pleasant. Having a hope for the future is therefore something which is a gift from God that we do not deserve. The Apostle Paul was very clear on this point:

> "For the wages of sin is death, but the free gift of God is eternal life in Christ Jesus our Lord." (Romans 6:23)

Salvation and the hope of life in God's kingdom are gifts which originate from Him. It is God who takes the initiative and chooses to offer salvation as His free gift to us. This is known as *grace*. One of the most popular definitions for grace is 'undeserved divine favour'. That means to say, it is something that God extends to us because He chooses to do so and because He wants to, not because He ought to or because He is in our debt. He wants to have a relationship with human beings and He wants it so much that He sent His own son as a sacrifice so that it can happen. This grace is undeserved and it is one of the most important concepts in scripture.

But this very important point does not mean that we sit back and do nothing. God takes the initiative, certainly – His hand is outstretched to us, as it were. But we have to *respond*; we have to choose whether to take His hand or not. We have to decide whether we will repent and turn from our own way to go God's way and we have to decide whether we will believe in what He has promised.

What must I do?

The Apostle Paul and his companion Silas once had occasion to preach to a jailer in the Greek town of Philippi. The instant the man realised the significance and urgency of Paul's words he asked a very important question. Notice both the directness of the question, and the significance of the answer:

"Then [the jailer] ... said, 'Sirs, what must I do to be saved?' And they said, 'Believe in the Lord Jesus, and you will be saved, you and your household.'" (Acts 16:30)

What is required on our part, then, is that we *believe* in the Gospel message – the things concerning the kingdom and the Lord Jesus Christ.

Along a similar vein, some people who were interested in Jesus' teachings once asked him this question:

"What must we do, to be doing the works of God?" (John 6:28)

This is a very natural and very human question. We tend to think that there must be something that we must *do* to earn or merit salvation, to show that we are worthy of being saved. But Jesus' answer to their question is deliberately paradoxical. He says:

> "This is the work of God, that you believe in him [Jesus] whom He [God] has sent." (John 6:29)

We wouldn't normally think of belief as being a 'work'. Belief is a state of mind, something that takes place (or doesn't) in the brain, whereas work is something tangible that you physically *do*. Jesus doesn't see it that way, however. The most important *work*, Jesus says, is to *believe*.

It isn't necessarily easy. In a world full of tangible things and experimental proof it can be hard to believe that God will one day send His son back to the earth to establish a kingdom of goodness and peace (to take just one important example). The very concept is so far removed from our everyday experience that it can seem like a dream or wish, something to comfort us rather than something which can withstand the cold, harsh scrutiny of rationality. But there are strong evidences for faith. Belief in God or in His purpose is not something which has no basis in fact or rationality; God has left ample evidence of Himself both within nature, in the unique record of the Bible, in His activities through history accurately predicted beforehand in the Bible (fulfilled prophecy), in the way in which Bible-based faith so perfectly fits our wants and needs as a species and provides the critical 'missing-link' in our lives, and in the evidence for the resurrection of Jesus. All of these strands of evidence, while not algebraic proof, help to build a strong evidence-based faith. Beyond that we need to open our minds to the possibility that what is possible to the Creator of the world is not limited by what we can see, nor by the things that we think we know. God is not limited by nature or by the rules we impose upon Him because He created nature and He created us.

Back to Abraham

It's hard to overstate the importance of having faith or belief in the Gospel message, a topic which marries perfectly with something which happened more than a thousand years before concerning someone named Abraham. We met Abraham in passing back in an earlier chapter – he was both the father of the Jews and many Arab peoples and someone to whom God made remarkable promises. The significance of Abraham in this context – the thing that the Bible singles out about him above all others – is his faith: his implicit belief and trust in what God said. Although Abraham did some incredible things like leaving his home to go to a land God would show him but which he had never seen, what was really special about him was his faith:

> "For what does the Scripture say? 'Abraham *believed* God, and it was counted to him as righteousness.'" (Romans 4:3)

Notice that this verse does not say that Abraham *was* righteous – he was a sinner, just like the rest of us. But he *believed God* and he did so against tremendous odds. It was *this* that marked him out and made him special. And because he believed God, God *counted it* to him for righteousness. That means God considered him as if he were righteous and treated him in that way – but He did this because of Abraham's belief rather than because of what was intrinsically the case! This is how important our belief is in God's sight.

> "Know then that it is those of faith [i.e., belief] who are the sons of Abraham ... So then, those who are of faith are blessed along with Abraham, the man of faith ... for in Christ Jesus you are all sons of God, through faith ... And if you are Christ's, then you are Abraham's offspring, heirs according to promise." (Galatians 3:7,9,26,29)

This passage may sound a bit complicated, but the basic message is actually quite simple: if we believe God like Abraham did then the promises God made to Abraham (about Jesus and about the kingdom) become our promises too. We inherit them because we have become Abraham's spiritual descendants by behaving and believing in the same way as he. This is extremely good news because these promises are ones which unlock the future both for the world at large and, if we believe, for us as individuals as well.

Chapter 30

Saying sorry

SAYING 'sorry' oughtn't to be so difficult – it's not like the words are hard to pronounce or that uttering them causes physical pain. Yet somehow saying sorry is categorically *not* easy, even though it's often exactly the right thing to do. It's embarrassing; it's emotionally painful; it hurts our pride. No one likes to admit they were wrong.

Where our relationship with God is concerned, however, saying sorry is exactly what we need to do. Whether we think of humanity at large or of our own individual lives, God has made the rules and we have broken them one way or another. We need to say that we're sorry, and mean it. This chapter is all about repentance and it leads on to another chapter about baptism, two vital steps by which God wants us to respond to the wonderful message of hope He has given.

Repentance

The Bible doesn't really use words like 'apologise' or 'say sorry', but it does have a lot to say about repenting, which amounts to a similar thing. Repentance is about realising that you were going one way (which was wrong), regretting it, saying you're sorry, and starting out in a new and better direction.

Let's take a look at some examples to see just how important this step is in beginning a relationship with God. Right at the beginning of Jesus' ministry, only fourteen verses into Mark's Gospel account of Jesus' life, we read this about how Jesus began his public mission:

> "Jesus came ... proclaiming the gospel of God, and saying, 'The time is fulfilled, and the kingdom of God is at hand; **repent and believe** in the gospel." (Mark 1:14,15)

Bound up with Jesus' teaching about the kingdom was a message of personal reform: a message that demanded a response from his audience – a message to repent and believe. Quite clearly, Jesus wanted his hearers to respond to his message by realising that the way they had been living their lives up to this point was inadequate; they needed to be sorry, and they needed to change. It's just the same if we look at the preaching of the apostles. Here is the Apostle Peter addressing a huge crowd shortly after Jesus' ascension:

> "**Repent** therefore, and turn again, that your sins may be blotted out, that times of refreshing may come from the presence of the Lord ..."   (Acts 3:19)

Notice that Peter connects repentance here with the idea of 'turning': it is as if his hearers' lives had been pointed in one direction and now needed to change so that they are pointed towards a new and better way. And that's exactly right. It's human nature to put self first and to look after number one, but that's not the way to please God. Instead, He asks us to be focused upon loving Him and our neighbour, telling us that *this* is the way to true happiness and fulfilment in life.

The burden of guilt

Initially, this message of repentance might seem hard to swallow. We might feel that we really haven't done anything that bad. Sure, we've upset people a few times; occasionally we might have been bad tempered or mean-spirited. But do we really need to make such a big deal of this repentance business?

If we do feel like that (and it's quite understandable) then it's probably a consequence of not really having got to grips with the problem of sin in the world *and the fact that every one of us is part of the problem*. You might find it helpful to revisit some of the material in chapters 12-15 if you feel that way.

The fact is that if you scratch beneath the surface most of us carry around with us the burden of a lot of guilt and disappointment. We might try to hide it away by not thinking about it, but most of us have things in our lives of which we're ashamed or where we carry a burden of regret. We might try to feel better about ourselves by blaming some external factor like our parents or our socio-economic background, but those burdens may still gnaw at us.

Keeping quiet about it, pretending the problem isn't there, or blaming someone else doesn't work at the end of the day. We need to own up to ourselves and to God and lay these things at Jesus' feet so that he may bear our burdens. While those we have hurt may or may not find it in themselves to forgive us, the fact is that God can and will. Whatever the guilt is that we carry, God can forgive us and take that burden away.

The beauty of forgiveness by God is that *all* sins can be washed away. We really can make a new start. This is exactly what God invites us to do, but we must begin the process by acknowledging where we are and by the act of repentance.

Chapter 31

Brand new start

OF course repentance is not *just* about saying you're sorry. We've all probably had the experience of witnessing someone saying they're sorry in such a way that it's very clear that they're actually *not* sorry at all! Needless to say, this isn't what God is looking for. Nor is He looking for us to say we're sorry only for us to carry on behaving in exactly the same way as if nothing had happened, without attempting to change a thing. He wants us to go forward trying to be different people to the way we were before we encountered Him, before we were aware of our need for repentance.

If we want to have a good relationship with God and to look forward to sharing in the wonderful hope He has offered, then what God requires is nothing less than a new start. God is right and He knows what is best for us. The first step in returning to Him is to recognise this to be true, to acknowledge our need for Him and the hope He offers, and to demonstrate that we're prepared to make that new start.

Baptism: showing we mean it

How do we show God that we really mean our repentance? How do we make a once-in-a-lifetime change from going our own way to trying to go God's? God asks us to do this by being *baptized*. Biblical Christianity has remarkably little ritual in it, but the rare exceptions are rendered all the more significant by the fact that they are not the norm. Baptism is one such very significant exception.

First lets address what baptism is, and then turn to the more important question of what it means and why it is important. Biblical baptism takes place when a person professes their faith in God and the Lord Jesus Christ before a witness or witnesses who share the same faith. They repent of their past sins and are then fully immersed or covered by water for a few seconds. It is a conscious step taken by a responsible person who understands God's message and plan and wants to show their commitment to it by turning from their old ways and beginning a new life in Him.

You'll notice, incidentally, that there's a big contrast between this type of baptism and the concept of the christening of a tiny baby. Christening isn't spoken about in the Bible at all, whereas Biblical baptism is an act which is carried out voluntarily by someone who is responsible enough for themselves to confess their sins, express their faith, and realise the significance of what they are doing.

What baptism means

Why does baptism matter? Because it is a symbolic way of connecting ourselves with Jesus' own death and resurrection. The immersion or complete covering by water is a symbolic 'burial' under the water. It speaks of a person surrendering and dying to their old way of life while the coming up out of the water speaks of a new beginning – a life now to be lived in the light of faith. Baptism represents us saying goodbye to our old way of life – turning our back on self-seeking and trying to survive by our own strength or smartness – laying aside the past and stepping forward into a brighter future as a member of God's family with the hope of eternal life in God's kingdom when Jesus returns.

The connection with Jesus' own death and resurrection is important. The Apostle Paul says that we are 'baptized into his death' (see Romans 6:2-6) – that is, we associate ourselves with him and his sacrifice through the ritual of baptism. It's not that Jesus died and was raised so that we don't have to go through the process; rather, he set the pattern as our representative and we follow in his footsteps. We don't *literally* die as he was literally crucified but we *symbolically* participate in his death through the act of baptism, recognising that the human way is not God's way. We surrender our lives as Christ surrendered his so that we may begin again. Christ's resurrection is also a pattern for us: just as he was raised from the dead so we rise from the water that has 'buried' us in baptism to begin a new and spiritually-focused life in God's sight. Of course we will still literally die one day (if Jesus' return doesn't come first), but the spiritual life we will have begun is a foretaste of that future day of resurrection when Jesus will return and we will literally be raised from the dead as he was, with the hope of joining him in a new life in God's kingdom.

The great news about baptism is that it doesn't matter what went before. God can forgive *anything* that we have done before and allow us to begin again if we turn to Him in sincerity and are baptized; while the consequences of our past actions may well remain, the sin is completely washed away. It is a genuine and exhilarating new beginning, a re-birth into a new way of life following the commandments of God, a new life as part of God's spiritual family.

Chapter 32

Passport to the future

THE transformation that God wants to take place in our lives when we receive and accept the Gospel message is profound. So fundamental, in fact, that some quite drastic metaphors are employed to describe it. One is the idea of citizenship: being a follower of Christ means carrying a different passport, if you will; it is as fundamental as being a citizen of a different country. It suggests a whole new set of priorities and responsibilities, a whole new way of living.

New citizenship

While our passports may still announce us to be British or German (or whatever it happens to be), the Bible speaks of us becoming 'citizens of heaven'. This symbolism of being a citizen of God's coming kingdom is an important driver for the behaviour of a disciple.

God and Jesus want us to prioritise spiritual or heavenly matters above everything else in life. Our first responsibility, in everything, is to God and to His son. Jesus asks us to strive to put our new citizenship, our new family obligations and our hope of the kingdom ahead of anything else:

> "Therefore do not be anxious, saying, 'What shall we eat?' or 'What shall we drink?' or 'What shall we wear?' ... your heavenly Father knows that you need them all. But seek first the kingdom of God and his righteousness, and all these things will be added to you." (Matthew 6:31-33)

Jesus also asked disciples to show the same kind of sacrificial love that he had shown in their interactions with other people. In asking this Jesus knew full well that he was asking them to go against their every instinct. He was deliberately setting a high bar which would constantly challenge everyone who attempted it – but then little that is truly worthwhile is easy. It is our human nature to defend and protect ourselves, to wish harm on those who harm us and to take care of those who are good to us. Jesus asks us to turn the tables on that kind of thinking. If God had given us only what we deserved, we should all be dead and there would be no hope. The whole point is that "while we were still sinners, Christ died for us" (Romans 5:8). God had mercy and love for us when in many respects we were unlovable. He asks us to show our appreciation of this point by trying to behave the same way:

> "But I say to you, love your enemies and pray for those who persecute you, so that you may be sons of your Father who is in heaven ... If you love those who love you, what reward do you have? Do not even the tax collectors do the same?"
>
> (Matthew 5:44-46)

This is nothing less than a complete paradigm shift, one which is both liberating and revolutionary. Jesus is telling us that we must start to configure the world and the possibilities for our behaviour within it in an entirely new and motivating way. We don't have to do what is 'normal' or what is 'natural'. We can instead try to do what is right and what is best.

Further implications of citizenship

A believer's new citizenship implies that they must try to behave appropriately as citizens, representatives, and even *ambassadors* of their new kingdom. If we are now citizens of a different kingdom with a changed nationality then that means that we don't really belong to or have the same involvement with our old country that we once did. Although other people will still consider us by the old norms, the fact is that our allegiance and primary loyalty has changed. We are not primarily British or Malaysian any more; in fact, we are in a way *foreigners* in Britain or Malaysia! This means that we'll no longer have the same level of participation in the affairs of the country in which we live.

There are practical consequences of living as a guest in a foreign country. First, we should live peaceably in the world, being respectful of the rulers and powers it has appointed and through which God is working (He works through evil regimes as well as good). The Bible therefore tells us that the servants of the Lord "must not strive" (2 Timothy 2:24, KJV), which excludes militant actions and other activist movements. We should pay our taxes (Jesus did – Matthew 17:24-27; 22:21), we should pay our debts (Romans 13:8) and keep our promises. We should not be troublemakers.

The only exception to the rule about obeying the laws and rulers of the land as a resident guest is when those laws bring us into conflict with the laws of God. In that case, as the Apostle Peter once eloquently put it, "We ought to obey God rather than men" (Acts 5:29, KJV; see also Acts 4:19).

Our main objective in life will not be to maximise our personal wealth, pleasure or gratification. Much of society's media may come to seem hollow and somewhat pointless when seen in this light. Instead of pandering to our lower instincts our focus will be on trying to lead a life which is fulfilling because it is focused on God and on others rather than on ourselves. It is when we tune our lives in that direction, in harmony with the kingdom which is to come, that we shall find a greater, more lasting happiness and fulfilment in life. This is, after all, what we were designed for.

Chapter 33

New family

WHILE it's true that there is a sense in which all human beings are God's children, by copying Adam's sins of selfishness and disobedience we've naturally associated ourselves more with Adam as our spiritual forefather rather than with God. Consequently it's natural and genetic that we inherit his nature: sinful, self-seeking, suffering, and tending towards death. Baptism is about disowning that legacy (though we still continue to suffer its consequences, if not its fate) and choosing to be part of *God's* family.

What does it all mean?

Effectively it's like being adopted from one family (the family of Adam) into another (the family of God) through the work of Jesus. Being part of this new family brings with it new privileges and new responsibilities:

> "For in Christ Jesus you are all sons of God, through faith. For as many of you as were baptized into Christ have put on Christ. There is neither Jew nor Greek, there is neither slave nor free, there is no male and female, for you are all one in Christ Jesus."
>
> (Galatians 3:26-29)

There are several key aspects to our new membership of God's family after baptism:

1. Our relationship with God as the head of the house, and our relationship with Jesus;
2. Our relationship with other members of the family;
3. Our relationship with those who are not family members.

Let's think about each of these in turn.

First, our relationship to God and Jesus. This is critical. As members of their family, we're meant to please and obey them, follow their commands and be good family representatives to those around. The first commandment – like the first commandment of the Law of Moses hundreds of years before – is that we should love God with all our heart, soul, strength and mind, and put Him first in our lives. We show that we love Him by making His commands our priority and by living in a way which will please Him, whether we're at work, with our families, or in any other situation.

A worldwide family

But what about our relationship with other believers who are also members of God's family? Meeting regularly and working with others who believe the same and share a common hope is an important component of the new life in Christ. While it's possible to live in isolation from other believers (in some cases there really may be no alternative), it's tremendously helpful to have the support and encouragement of other like-minded people. The value of having the rough edges and corners knocked off each other through the sometimes trying task of having to get along is also not to be underestimated; it may not always be pleasant, but it is probably good for us!

But what constitutes God's family, and which believers should we meet with? Will any church do? Does it have to be a particular one, and does this imply that other churches or denominations are *not* part of God's true family?

Ultimately, of course, these are questions for God to decide. He will be the judge of who is in His family and who is not. But that does not quite get us off the hook. We still each have a personal responsibility to choose wisely and carefully the right church or community to join. It is important not to select purely on the basis of what 'feels' right, what seems most modern or sophisticated, or which church has the people we happen to get on with the best. God places a premium both on what people *understand* about Him (that is, whether beliefs are true or false), and also on what they *do* on the basis of that understanding. In an earlier age there might have been a tendency for people to be more concerned with the former, whereas now the pendulum has probably swung more towards the latter. Both are important, however.

We each have a responsibility to examine the Bible for ourselves and to compare its teachings with the various Christian churches and denominations we might meet, to decide whether or not they are really teaching Bible truth. There is an example of some baptized believers in the Bible who discovered they didn't really properly understand important aspects of the Bible's message when they were initially baptized and who were therefore baptized again (this is recorded in Acts 19). It is a very surprising incident but it shows that what one believes and what one's church teaches really does matter. It's also important that a church that teaches the right things also tries to *do* them: worshipping God sincerely and wholeheartedly, supporting one another whatever our abilities and disabilities, and being involved in good works both within and without the immediate group of believers. [1]

Breaking bread and fellowship

Once you have been baptized into a community that you believe comes as close as possible to Bible hope and practice, it's a good idea to get as involved as you can. The word 'fellowship' is an important Bible concept, and this means being at one with your brothers and sisters (the other members of your spiritual family). Together we all

---

1 The Christadelphians, the community who sponsored this book, are a worldwide family of believers who meet regularly around a common, Bible-based faith in the Lord Jesus and the hope of the kingdom. Like any other community it has its faults – it has human beings in it, after all. But it also has tremendous strengths, in particular its back-to-the-Bible focus; its Biblical understanding of God, man, the Lord Jesus, and the future hope of the kingdom; its warm, family-like fellowship, and its worldwide preaching mission. You can find out more about the Christadelphians at the back of this book.

share a common need of salvation, and we need the support of one another as we try to journey towards God's kingdom.

Fellowship involves things like reading and studying the Bible together, praying together, worshipping together, being involved in acts of charity, care or preaching, gaining help in tackling difficulties and problems, supporting the weak and rejoicing with the strong. One of the most important acts of fellowship is the breaking of bread and drinking of wine ('communion') in memory of the sacrifice of the Lord Jesus. The first century apostles carried out this simple act of remembrance on the first day of the week (Sunday). It is a simple yet powerful memorial of Jesus' life, his work and sacrifice, and his death and resurrection. The bread, which is passed around so that each baptized member can break off and eat a small piece, is a symbol of Jesus' body – a life given in service to his Father – and of the unity that believers share in him. The wine, also passed around so that each baptized member can take a sip, is a symbol of Jesus' blood which was shed as a sacrifice for sin.

The world around

Continuing the family symbolism, there are also responsibilities to those who may not believe in God or have not committed to a new life in Christ through baptism – responsibilitles *outside* the family. During Jesus' ministry he preached the Gospel, but he also healed the sick. The pairing of these two elements as a summary of his ministry is important. Jesus brought a message about the future and about the spiritual repentance and reform which was necessary to prepare for it. But he also helped people in the here-and-now by healing their sicknesses and bringing real relief. He knew they would get sick again and that the relief he brought was only temporary, but it was important for him to provide it nevertheless. He clearly cared about the circumstances and suffering of others and did what he could to help.

Similarly, in the Old Testament, it was a crucial part of the Law of Moses that the Jews should look after the poor and the disadvantaged, the widows and the fatherless, and those who had no one else to help them. These responsibilities remain important today. This suggests that acts of kindness towards others are entirely in keeping with the spirit of the Bible (whether this be towards our neighbours and acquaintances, or on a wider scale through charities or volunteer work). By helping with such things we will not solve the world's problems in any absolute sense – only God can do that by sending Jesus to set up His kingdom – but we will show that we care, and that we appreciate the care which God has shown towards us. While the Gospel message is the only thing that can *really* save men and women in any ultimate sense, the fact remains that through ordinary, everyday acts of kindness we shall be showing our concern and compassion and following a sound scriptural example. Jesus told a famous parable, the parable of the Good Samaritan, to remind us of our responsibility to care for those we wouldn't normally think of, the person we might be cautious or reluctant to help.

The Apostle James summed it up this way:

"Religion that is pure and undefiled before God, the Father, is this: to visit orphans and widows in their affliction, and to keep oneself unstained from the world."   (James 1:27)

Chapter 34

Time to get ready

IF you have made it all the way through the book to these final chapters then we'll have travelled on a significant journey together. We began by thinking about what we called the Big Questions of life, and reflected on how valuable it would be if we could find consistent, sensible answers to them that we could really trust. While it would be a frustrating and unreliable exercise to find such answers amongst the many human voices out there clamouring to be heard or by looking on the internet, we found that the Bible not only claimed to provide the answers to these questions as the word of God but also has a track record to back up those claims which is completely unlike any other book that has ever been written.

The Bible presents a clear and logical vision of where the world has come from, where it is going, and what our purpose is within it. While human 'experts' can't even agree on what is the best diet, the Bible is definitive on all the fundamental questions of life – the ones which really matter yet which, paradoxically, we often don't stop to take the time to think about. When we think about the incredible universe we live in it makes total sense to believe that there is a supernatural creator outside of time and space, a divine mind who brought it all into being. Only that way can we find a truly satisfying explanation for the data, the laws, the rationality, and the many wonders in nature – and only then do the truly remarkable capabilities of the human mind truly makes sense, for they are a reflection of the one in whose image they were made.

When we understand God's 'prime directive' to fill the world with His glory and when we think about His purpose in creating human beings with free will but who are meant to be focused upon Him and engage in relationships with Him, the riddle of human existence starts to become clear. We begin to understand the paradox at the heart of our nature and the potential and longing that most of us feel for something better than this life. We become aware that we need to become in tune with Him – to re-establish that connection damaged through sin – in order to find our true place in the world.

Problems and solutions

The price of human free will is a high one – not only does it mean the power to do good; it also carries with it the power to hurt and to harm, the power to reject God and go one's own way, thinking that we know better than Him. It has led to all sorts of problems – *every* problem, in fact, that humans face both as a society and as individuals. While most religions and philosophies don't really have a convincing or sufficient account of human evil – they don't really grasp the nettle when thinking about the powers at stake in human nature – the Bible contains a clear and simple account of this central yet ugly fact about us and has had a perfect solution from the very beginning. Truly knowing what the problem is that needs to be solved is a crucial first step (much better than trying to pretend there isn't really an issue or living under the vague hope that things might gradually improve). We saw, in fact, that there are two particular problems that need to be addressed – the self-seeking and sin that takes place in human hearts at the individual level (unpleasant as it may seem, *we* are each part of that universal problem), and the society-wide problems that result and which need addressing on a global scale.

What we have is a *systemic* problem. Just as the Global Financial Crisis was systemic in that it affected all financial institutions whether or not they had actually created or owned any of the toxic assets that threatened to undermine the financial world, so too the problem of sin is systemic – it pervades the whole system of human interactions, our whole existence, whether or not we ourselves have personally committed this or that act of wrongdoing. We recognise the potential for greed, envy, thoughtlessness and cruelty within ourselves and we therefore know their power for harm when they are unchecked. We can spot the connection between what is wrong with society at large and what is wrong in our own hearts, and it becomes abundantly apparent that a comprehensive solution is needed.

It is in a sense a relief just to get this far: to correctly identify the fundamental problem that human beings are grappling with. But if it is a relief to identify the problem, how much more to know the solution! God has specifically and purposefully planned a way to address both individual sin and the global problems of our society. This solution is encapsulated in the Gospel message: the things concerning the kingdom of God and the name of the Lord Jesus.

The things concerning ...

How can human beings as sinful, dying creatures find their way back to God? The answer is that they can't find their own way back and they were never meant to – instead, God has found it for them. He did it by sending Jesus, His own son, as His perfect ambassador and representative – the one who pointed the way for us to follow. The coming of Jesus and the great work that he would do was promised right through the Old Testament scriptures dating from thousands of years ago. It was predicted in the amazing promises that God made to Adam and Eve, to Abraham, to Moses, and to David (not to mention many others we didn't have time to consider). Jesus would be born of a woman, just as we all are, fully human and a participant in our temptable and dying nature. But he would also be the Son of God, more in tune with God's ways and capable of perfectly representing Him than any of us would ever be. Jesus taught a message of repentance and reform, that men and women should seek first the kingdom of God and follow the narrow way of behaviour and faith which leads there. There simply isn't anything more worthwhile to concentrate on in life than this.

By his sacrificial death Jesus showed his love, his willingness to give the most precious thing he could, and his preparedness to take on the burden of our sins, nailing them to his cross. The Father showed *His* love in providing and giving His most precious son to illustrate both the extent of His love and mercy, but also the awfulness of sin, where it leads, and what it deserves. Through Jesus' amazing resurrection from the dead there is hope for all of us both for a new life in Christ today, and for the resurrection to a new and higher level of existence in God's kingdom.

Speaking of the kingdom, it has always been God's plan to establish His kingdom upon the earth and to fill the earth with His knowledge and glory. This is where the world is going; this is its bright future. God spoke of this to Abraham, He spoke of it to David, and He spoke of it repeatedly through the mouths of the prophets whose writings make up around a third of the entire Bible. The future kingdom of God in which Jesus will return and reign as king – the solution to the mess, mismanagement and global problems that man has caused – is a message of hope of which the Bible never tires. It is the very essence of God's purpose and plan and now is the time to get ready for it.

Chapter 35

Next steps

OUR responsibility in the light of all this is to make a response to God's offer of salvation. To do that we need to examine the evidence for God and the Bible, we need to read it, and we need to make a judgement about whether we believe it and whether we want to be part of it. It is the most amazing message the world has ever known, and if we *do* want to participate then we need to do something about it.

This book has only scratched the surface, both in terms of introducing the evidence for the world view the Bible presents and in terms of outlining Bible hope. There is much more depth to each of the themes we've discovered, and many other important topics and teachings which tie into what we have considered. A selection of materials to help take things further are mentioned in Appendix 2 (page 137).

The response

What God is looking for from those who want to serve Him is a response of faith. His hand is outstretched, and He wants us to trust Him and to take it. Jesus put it like this:

> "Take my yoke upon you, and learn from me, for I am gentle and lowly in heart, and you will find rest for your souls. For my yoke is easy, and my burden is light." (Matthew 11:29,30)

The world can be lonely and it can be harsh; but if we truly understand God's purpose and His great desire to save men and women if only they turn to Him, then this becomes an incredible force of comfort and purpose in a believer's life. God is *always* there; He will never leave us unless we choose to banish Him. He will care and He will watch over us. As Jesus also said,

> "Fear not, little flock, for it is your Father's good pleasure to give you the kingdom." (Luke 12:32)

As our faith and understanding of God grows we'll be in a position to make a decision about wiping the slate of our old lives clean, potentially obeying Jesus' command to be baptized for the forgiveness of sins and beginning a new life in him. As we do so, we shall be joining a new family and we shall be receiving a new citizenship. These will be the hallmarks of the new way of life that we shall want to try to lead, a life focused upon God and upon pleasing Him. We shall find that this new focus was the 'missing piece' in the jigsaw puzzle of our previous lives. We shall find it a tremendous source of hope and courage as we face the future.

Waiting for Christ's return

So what of that future? God has made it clear where we are headed. Men and women will not continue their fumbling attempts at leading society for much longer. The geopolitical events taking place in the world today are signs that the return of Jesus is near and that God's kingdom will soon be set up. The days that remain are an opportunity to prepare for that magnificent time.

We need to take action, and we can start today. Here are some suggestions from the Apostle Paul:

> "I appeal to you therefore, brothers, by the mercies of God, to present your bodies as a living sacrifice, holy and acceptable to God, which is your spiritual worship. Do not be conformed to this world, but be transformed by the renewal of your mind ..."
> (Romans 12:1,2)

> "Whatever you do, work heartily, as for the Lord and not for men." (Colossians 3:23)

Jesus will return soon. True fulfilment in life both at that time and now is not to be found in business; nor is to be found in pleasure and self-seeking. Business and pleasure and family and all the other activities we engage in can each of them be deeply rewarding and stimulating in their place; many of the opportunities we have in life – and life itself – are wonderful gifts from God to be enjoyed and appreciated. But they are not the ultimate reality; they are not what life is truly about. Jesus told us to seek first God's kingdom, and if we do, the other things that we need will be provided for us according to God's will.

We only live this life once, so it's worth taking the time to understand what it's all about. And it's worth making sure we've got our priorities right. A new life in God's family, trusting in Him, hoping for and seeking the coming kingdom which He has promised from the very beginning, is a life of purpose, a life of joy, destiny and commitment. It is a life of meaning.

Appendices

Appendix 1

The authority – the remarkable credentials of the Bible

JEWS and Christians have long claimed the Bible to be God's book, the one through which He has communicated with humans about Himself and His purpose. But is this really true – are we right to turn to the Bible for answers, and why should we turn to this book rather than to one of the other religious texts that exist in the world for the answers to our questions?

These are very fair questions. What *is* so special about the Bible and why does it polarize opinion so much? What is the evidence for making the claim that it can be trusted to provide reliable answers to life's big questions?

In this appendix we review seven points which give a taster for the Bible's uniqueness in world literature and which support the claim that it is indeed the very place we need to look to find out more about God and His ways. These points, when considered in more depth, combine into a powerful case for believing that the Bible must indeed be the word of God.

SEVEN UNIQUE FEATURES OF THE BIBLE:

1 WORLD'S BEST-SELLER. First, it's famous. The Bible is the world's best-selling book – translated into more languages and distributed more widely than any other book in the world. This does not prove it to be true but it shows that there must be something very remarkable about it. What is it about the Bible that has made people so eager to translate and distribute it?

Why do so many people buy it? Why do millions of ordinary people *still* read it today, thousands of years after it was written? There are very, very few books you can say that about.

2 **DARING CLAIMS.** Second, the Bible claims to be the word of God, able to save people's lives. Again, there haven't been many books in history that have dared to make that claim because as soon as a book sets itself up as speaking for God, people are lining up to prove it wrong. But the Bible insists. More than eight hundred times it uses phrases like 'this is what the Lord says ...' or 'The word of the Lord came to me, saying ...' These are bold, bold claims. And the Bible stands alone as the one book, more than any other, upon which men and women have sought to base their lives and for which they have been prepared to die.

More than merely reporting the words of God, however, the Bible claims to *be* the word of God, living and powerful, and able to save people. It's not that the Bible merely *contains* the word of God (as though some parts are optional or sub-standard); it says that it *is* the word of God – in all its parts – and hundreds of thousands of people take those claims seriously and find their lives much richer as a result. It tells us the facts we need about God, ourselves, and God's plan. It tells us where we've gone wrong and shows us how to do things better. It takes us to a higher level of living, more in tune with God and His ways. It's pretty dark out there – the world is a confusing place with all kinds of challenges – but the Bible can be a guide, a source of direction, a light to show us the way.

3 **UNITY IN DIVERSITY.** No other book has been written in quite the same way as the Bible. It's actually not one book at all, but a library of sixty-six books, written by around forty different authors over a period of more than 1,500 years. It grew over time until it reached completion roughly two thousand years ago.

The story and manner of the Bible's composition is unique. Yet despite its unparalleled diversity (it contains history, law, poetry, letters, parables, essays) and its unique history of formation, it has an amazing consistency, coherence, and singleness of purpose. There is a clear overarching message – a golden thread which unites it despite the unique way in which it was written by so many people over so many years. Most Bible believers have a personal favourite reason for believing the Bible, and this is a common one. Just like when you take a microscope and focus in on a blade of grass or a flower, you see incredible beauty that you had no idea was there when looking with the naked eye, so it is with the Bible. Its intricacy and its power, as well as its connectedness and consistency, is very powerful evidence.

4 ACCURACY OF PRESERVATION. When you read the Bible, how do you know you are reading what the original writers actually wrote? After all, you're reading a document that is between 2,000 and 3,500 years old, written in completely different languages, before there were electronic backups or printing presses.

It turns out that there is no other book in the world of remotely comparable age which we know has been transmitted through history with such accuracy. This feature is unparalleled in any other ancient book. Is this just a fluke of history, or did God plan it that way?

Here are just a few of many statistics to give a flavour of this point. How many ancient copies are there of Homer's *Iliad*, another very significant ancient work? The answer is around 650, and the oldest full manuscript dates from about 1,400 years after the supposed time of original composition. Now the *Iliad* is considered a relatively well-preserved work, but that's quite a length of time that passed – 1,400 years – between its original composition and our oldest complete copy. Who knows what happened in between?

What about the New Testament, by comparison? Instead of the *Iliad*'s 650 copies, we have around 24,000 manuscripts and manuscript fragments, the earliest of which date from within a century or two of original writing! In fact, even if we had *no* manuscripts, we could actually recreate virtually the entire New Testament from quotations that other writers made from it hundreds of years ago. There is no other book from ancient times which has been preserved with such accuracy. Coincidence? We have to judge for ourselves but suffice it to say that there is more uncertainty about the text of Shakespeare, writing about 450 years ago, than there is about the New Testament.

5 **SURVIVAL.** The Bible has survived. This might not sound that amazing, but it is. Over the centuries people have had plenty of motivation for destroying the Bible or disprove it (that way they don't have to do what it says!). There have been many attempts to do so. The French philosopher Voltaire claimed that within a hundred years of his death, God and the Bible would be completely discredited, and no one would read the Bible any more. In fact, within fifty years of his death, the Geneva Bible society had, in a strange quirk of history, taken ownership of Voltaire's printing press and were using it to print Bibles to send all over the world!

In the face of attempts to burn and ban it, to torch its translators and printers at the stake, the Bible lives on. Today, critics are more likely to try to attempt to marginalize, dismiss or ridicule the Bible (often without having read it) – yet still people read it. It is a book that will not lie down.

6 **TELLING THE FUTURE.** The Bible has told and continues to tell the future. No other major world religion can lay claim to evidence of this kind from prophecy. The birth and death of Jesus were predicted hundreds of years before he was born, and the Bible has many remarkable prophecies about the Jewish nation (to whom the Old Testament was originally given) and some of the world empires and nations of the past.

It's important to realise that Bible prophecies are not vague and general like, say, the prophecies of Nostradamus. They are specific, and many of them have been fulfilled. They give evidence that other key elements of God's plan will indeed come to pass as He has said. They help us to understand that when God offers hope for the future, He knows what He is talking about. Fulfilled prophecy is a big subject but one well worth looking into for some very concrete evidence not only of the truth of the Bible but also of God's involvement in the affairs of human history. [1]

7 IT MAKES SENSE. Finally, there is the explanatory power of the Bible. The Bible provides a logical and credible explanation of why the world is the way it is, what human nature is like, and what has gone wrong – an explanation which many feel is the most compelling way of understanding ourselves and our world. The Bible explains the emptiness and lack of purpose or direction that men and women sometimes feel in today's world. And it tells us what we need to do in order to put things right and get back into a good relationship with God. Every reader has to decide whether there is another book or theory out there which fits the facts so well.

Putting it all together

There can be no doubt at all that the Bible stands unique among the literature of the world. No sensible person could seriously dispute this. Whether it is the word of God, revealing His plan and purpose is a more complicated question, and one that has to be decided by a careful consideration of the evidence and by first-hand experience of what the Bible says. It's hard not to agree, however, that there is enough evidence to at least take the Bible's claims seriously and see what it has to say. This is what we have been doing during the course of this book, looking at its answers to life's big questions.

It's worth taking just a few more moments to establish a couple of further points about exactly what kind of book we are dealing with when we open the Bible. We've already noted that in a way the Bible

---

1 You'll find some suggestions on where to find out more about Bible prophecy in the next appendix (page 137).

is more like a library than a single book – yet there is a key connection between all of its component parts. The parts only really make full sense and fit together when you have the rest of the collection; they are designed to belong together.

The sixty-six books of the Bible can be further divided into two parts: the Hebrew Bible or Old Testament (the first four-fifths of the Bible, accounting for thirty-nine of its sixty-six books), and the New Testament (the final fifth and the remaining twenty-seven books). The Old Testament charts the story of the world from the beginning of creation and puts particular focus on the few thousand years of history preceding the Lord Jesus, with its final part being written approximately 400 years before his birth. The Old Testament is held in esteem by both Jews, Christians and Muslims. For Judaism it represents the primary revelation of God to man (Judaism does not believe that Jesus is the promised Messiah, so it has no truck with the New Testament), while many Christians make the mistake of focusing so much on the New Testament that they miss how integral the Old Testament is to God's over-arching purpose with the world. In fact the whole Bible is essential – both the Old Testament and the New.

In many ways the Old Testament can be seen as presenting the questions to which the New Testament provides the answer in its description of the work and teaching of the Lord Jesus Christ. The Old Testament is vital because it presents so much important teaching about God and how He has dealt with the world and about His plans for the future, but it doesn't really make sense without the New Testament. It is only when Jesus comes onto the scene that the Old Testament suddenly springs into high definition and starts to make full sense because God's great solution to the thorny but critical problems of the Old Testament can now be seen in all its splendour.

The story and the thread

It's essential to understand that the Bible is largely *narrative* – that is, it presents a history: a spiritual history of God's interaction with the world which includes key characters and events who we will need to get to know over time. It isn't a theory book or a book primarily consisting of rules or abstract reflections. There is a narrative backbone, right from our first spiritual ancestors, Adam and Eve, through to God's interaction with His chosen people the Jews (a relationship He has used to illustrate to the wider world the way in which He engages with human beings at large), through to the life and work of His only begotten son Jesus, and then on to the work of the early apostles who spread that message throughout the world.

It is a book, therefore, of real people and real events – but in all these events there are lessons to be learned about God and His ways and His plans for the future. God engages in real-world history, reaching into the affairs of men and women to make Himself available. By examining and learning from these interactions we come to understand the real-life nature of faith and hope not through abstract propositions but as they are lived out in the lives of real people. We are not dealing with woolly or merely theoretical material when we open the Bible, therefore; we are dealing with concrete events, real people's lives, and the unfolding reality of God's grand scheme. The Bible is united and brought together by the idea of *promises* – wonderful promises that God has made to men and women and which are still relevant today. It is a record of the repeated and insistent promises that God has made to men and women and the conditions which are associated with them. It charts the unfolding fulfilment of those promises and in doing so it provides us with confidence that God will continue to deliver on what He has said and will ultimately fill the world with His glory.

Appendix 2

Further information

TO help explore some of the topics raised in this book you may like to consider the following.

Available free of charge

A full range of reading material is available from the Christadelphian Auxiliary Lecturing Society.

- **Postal address:** Freepost, The Christadelphians
- **Online:** (www.thechristadelphians.org.uk or www.the christadelphian.com – search for 'CALS')

Titles available include:

- **Hole, S.** – *Introducing the Christadelphians* (8 pages).
- **Morgan, O. T.** – *The God of the Bible* (32 pages).
- **Morgan, O. T.** – *What's so special about Jesus?* (19 pages).
- **Parry, J.** – *Bible Prophecy* (22 pages).
- **Walker, J.** – *The Case for Christianity* (24 pages).

Further information can be found at www.lifes-big-questions.org.

Available to buy

- **Morison, F.** – *Who Moved the Stone?* (192 pages; Authentic Media).
- **Tennant, H. A.** – *What the Bible Teaches* (304 pages; The Christadelphian Magazine and Publishing Association).